Bond

Assessment Papers

Fourth papers in
Maths

J M Bond and
Andrew Baines

Nelson Thornes

First published in 1973 by:
Thomas Nelson and Sons Ltd

This edition published in 2007 by:
Nelson Thornes Ltd
Delta Place
27 Bath Road
CHELTENHAM
GL53 7TH
United Kingdom

09 10 11 / 10 9 8 7 6 5

A catalogue record for this book is available from the British Library

ISBN 978 0 7487 8117 1

Page make-up by Tech Set Ltd

Printed and bound in Egypt by Sahara Printing Company

Before you get started

What is Bond?

This book is part of the Bond Assessment Papers series for maths, which provides **thorough and continuous practice of all the key maths content** from ages five to thirteen. Bond's maths resources are ideal preparation for many different kinds of tests and exams – from SATs to 11+ and other secondary school selection exams.

How does the scope of this book match real exam content?

Fourth and *More fourth papers* are the core Bond 11+ books. Each paper is **pitched at the level of a typical 11+ exam** and covers the key maths a child would be expected to learn. The papers are also in line with other selective exams for this age group. The coverage is matched to the National Curriculum and the National Numeracy Strategy and will also **provide invaluable preparation for Key Stage 2 SATs**. One of the key features of Bond Assessment Papers is that each one practises **a wide variety of skills and question types** so that children are always challenged to think – and don't get bored repeating the same question type again and again. We think that variety is the key to effective learning. It helps children 'think on their feet' and cope with the unexpected.

What does the book contain?

- **24 papers** – each one contains 50 questions.

- **Tutorial links throughout** – [B 7] – this icon appears in the margin next to the questions. It indicates links to the relevant section in *How to do ... 11+ Maths*, our invaluable subject guide that offers explanations and practice for all core question types.

- **Scoring devices** – there are score boxes in the margins and a Progress Chart on page 64. The chart is a visual and motivating way for children to see how they are doing. It also turns the score into a percentage that can help decide what to do next.

- **Next Steps Planner** – advice on what to do after finishing the papers can be found on the inside back cover.

- **Answers** – located in an easily-removed central pull-out section. If you lose your answers, please email cservices@nelsonthornes.com for another copy.

How can you use this book?

One of the great strengths of Bond Assessment Papers is their flexibility. They can be used at home, in school and by tutors to:

- set **timed formal practice** tests – allow about 30 minutes per paper in line with standard 11+ demands. Reduce the suggested time limit by five minutes to practise working at speed.

- provide **bite-sized chunks** for regular practice.

- **highlight strengths and weaknesses** in the core skills.

- identify **individual needs**.

- set **homework**.

- follow **a complete 11+ preparation strategy** alongside *The Parents' Stress-free Guide to the 11+* (see below).

It is best to start at the beginning and work through the papers in order. Calculators should not be used. Remind children to check whether each answer needs a unit of measurement before they start a test. If units of measurement are not included in answers that require them, they will lose marks for those questions. To ensure that children can practise including them in their answers, units of measurement have been omitted after the answer rules for some questions. If you are using the book as part of a careful run-in to the 11+, we suggest that you also have two other essential Bond resources close at hand:

How to do ... 11+ Maths: the subject guide that explains all the question types practised in this book. Use the cross-reference icons to find the relevant sections.

The Parents' Stress-free Guide to the 11+: the step-by-step guide to the whole 11+ experience. It clearly explains the 11+ process, provides guidance on how to assess children, helps you to set complete action plans for practice and explains how you can use the *Fourth* and *More fourth papers* in Maths as part of a strategic run-in to the exam.

See the inside front cover for more details of these books.

What does a score mean and how can it be improved?

It is unfortunately impossible to guarantee that a child will pass the 11+ exam if they achieve a certain score on any practice book or paper. Success on the day depends on a host of factors, including the scores of the other children sitting the test. However, we can give some guidance on what a score indicates and how to improve it.

If children colour in the Progress Chart on page 64, this will give an idea of present performance in percentage terms. The Next Steps Planner inside the back cover will help you to decide what to do next to help a child progress. It is always valuable to go over wrong answers with children. If they are having trouble with any particular question type, follow the tutorial links to *How to do ... 11+ Maths* for step-by-step explanations and further practice.

Don't forget the website...!

Visit www.assessmentpapers.co.uk for lots of advice, information and suggestions on everything to do with Bond, the 11+ and helping children to do their best.

Key words

Some special maths words are used in this book. You will find them **in bold** each time they appear in the papers. These words are explained here.

acute angle an angle that is less than a right angle

coordinates the two numbers, the first horizontal the second vertical, that plot a point on a grid, e.g. (3, 2)

factor the factors of a number are numbers that divide into it, e.g. 1, 2, 4 and 8 are all factors of 8

kite a four-sided shape that looks like a stretched diamond

lowest term the simplest you can make a fraction, e.g. $\frac{4}{10}$ reduced to the lowest term is $\frac{2}{5}$

mean one kind of average. You find the mean by adding all the scores together and dividing by the number of scores, e.g. the mean of 1, 3 and 8 is 4

median one kind of average, the middle number of a set of numbers after being ordered from lowest to highest, e.g. the median of 1, 3 and 8 is 3 e.g. the median of 7, 4, 6 and 9 is 6.5 (halfway between 6 and 7)

mixed number a number that contains a whole number and a fraction, e.g. $5\frac{1}{2}$ is a mixed number

mode one kind of average. The most common number in a set of numbers, e.g. the mode of 2, 3, 2, 7, 2 is 2

obtuse angle an angle that is more than 90° and not more than 180°

parallelogram a four-sided shape that has all its opposite sides equal and parallel

polygon a closed shape with many sides

prime factor the factors of a number that are also prime numbers, e.g. the prime factors of 12 are 2 and 3

prime number any number that can only be divided by itself or 1. 2, 3 and 7 are prime numbers. (Note that 1 is not a prime number.)

quotient the answer if you divide one number by another, e.g. the quotient of 12 ÷ 4 is 3

range the difference between the largest and smallest of a set of numbers, e.g. the range of 1, 2, 5, 3, 6, 8 is 7

reflex angle an angle that is bigger than 180°

rhombus a four-sided shape, like a squashed square, that has all its sides of equal length and its opposite sides parallel

trapezium a four-sided shape that has just one pair of parallel sides

vertex, vertices the point where two or more edges or sides in a shape meet

Paper 1

1–5 Here is a pie chart which shows how Joanna spent yesterday evening between 6 p.m. and 8 p.m.

Joanna was watching TV for _____ min, doing homework for _____ min, reading for

_____ min, washing up for _____ min and was on the computer for _____ min.

6–8 What is the average (**mean**) of the following numbers?

7 4 6 8 5 _____   3 2 7 _____   4 4 6 2 _____

9 Make 999 ten times as large.   _____

In each of the following lines, underline the smallest number and put a ring round the largest number.

10–11 $\frac{5}{8}$ $\frac{3}{4}$ $\frac{7}{8}$ $\frac{6}{8}$ $\frac{1}{2}$

12–13 3.07   3.7   37   3.007   0.307

14–15 $\frac{15}{3}$ $\frac{12}{6}$ $\frac{27}{9}$ $\frac{8}{2}$ $\frac{10}{10}$

16–17 0.125 $\frac{1}{2}$ 0.25 $\frac{7}{8}$ 0.75

18–19 $\frac{3}{4}$ of 12 $\frac{5}{7}$ of 14 $\frac{2}{3}$ of 9 $\frac{2}{5}$ of 10 $\frac{1}{2}$ of 16

20 Write in figures: one hundred and two thousand and twenty-one.   _____

21–24

| 17 | 21 | 39 | 45 | × 10 | − 1 |

What is the size of the smaller angle:

25 between 1 and 3?   _____

26 between 2 and 7?   _____

27 between 7 and 11?   _____

B 14
B 3
5
B 15
3
B 1
1
B 10
B 11
10
B 1
1
B 9
4
B 17
3

2

28–29 John used this decision tree to sort paint. What is missing from the tree? Fill in the gaps.

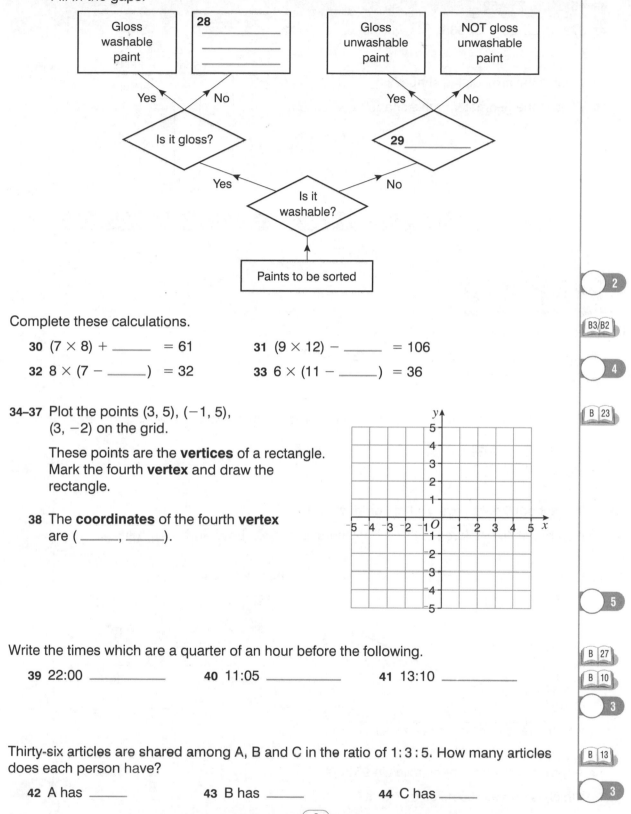

Complete these calculations.

30 $(7 \times 8) +$ _____ $= 61$

31 $(9 \times 12) -$ _____ $= 106$

32 $8 \times (7 -$ _____ $) = 32$

33 $6 \times (11 -$ _____ $) = 36$

34–37 Plot the points (3, 5), (−1, 5), (3, −2) on the grid.

These points are the **vertices** of a rectangle. Mark the fourth **vertex** and draw the rectangle.

38 The **coordinates** of the fourth **vertex** are (_____ , _____).

Write the times which are a quarter of an hour before the following.

39 22:00 _____

40 11:05 _____

41 13:10 _____

Thirty-six articles are shared among A, B and C in the ratio of 1 : 3 : 5. How many articles does each person have?

42 A has _____

43 B has _____

44 C has _____

Put a sign in each space to make these calculations correct.

B2/B3

45 45 _____ 7 = 52   **46** 33 _____ 3 = 11

47 678 _____ 56 = 37 968   **48** 90 _____ 5 = 18

4

B 20

49 What is the area of this shape?   _____ cm²

50 What is the perimeter of this shape?   _____ cm

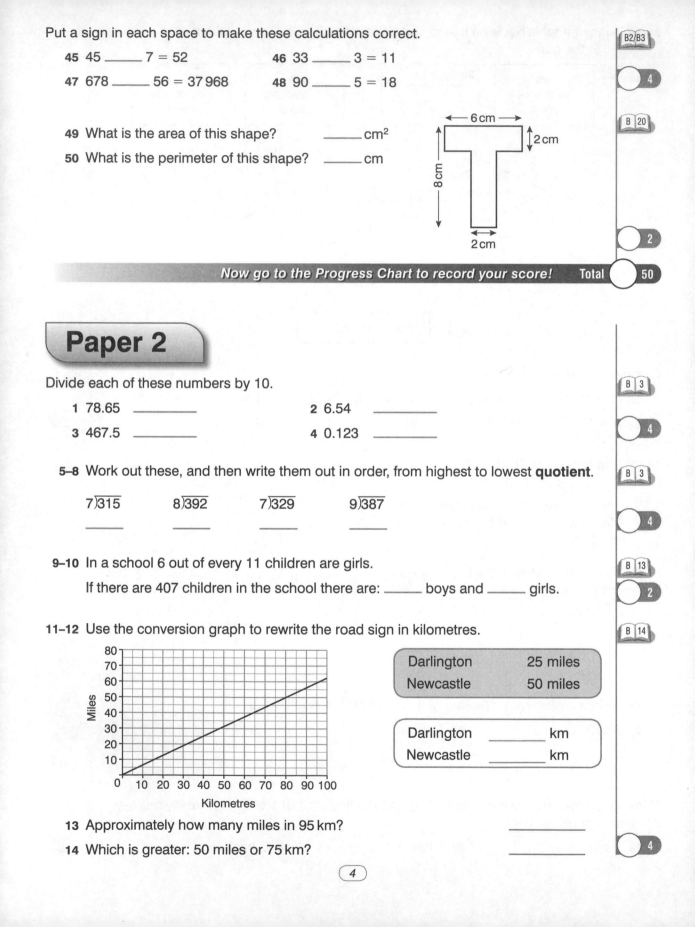

← 6 cm →

2 cm

8 cm

2 cm

2

Now go to the Progress Chart to record your score!   **Total**   50

Paper 2

Divide each of these numbers by 10.

B 3

1 78.65   _____   **2** 6.54   _____

3 467.5   _____   **4** 0.123   _____

4

5–8 Work out these, and then write them out in order, from highest to lowest **quotient**.

B 3

7)315   8)392   7)329   9)387

_____   _____   _____   _____

4

9–10 In a school 6 out of every 11 children are girls.

B 13

If there are 407 children in the school there are: _____ boys and _____ girls.

2

11–12 Use the conversion graph to rewrite the road sign in kilometres.

B 14

| Darlington | 25 miles |
| Newcastle | 50 miles |

| Darlington | _____ km |
| Newcastle | _____ km |

13 Approximately how many miles in 95 km?   _____

14 Which is greater: 50 miles or 75 km?   _____

4

Put a sign in each space to make these calculations correct.

15 74 _____ 5 = 14.8   **16** 74 _____ 5 = 79

17 74 _____ 5 = 69   **18** 74 _____ 5 = 370

There are six balls, numbered 1 to 6, in a bag.

19 What is the probability that I will draw out an even-numbered ball? _____

20 What is the probability that I will draw out the 5? _____

21 What is the probability that I will draw out an odd-numbered ball? _____

22–24 Put a circle around each **prime number**.

    3   4   5   6   7

25 What number is midway between 18 and 42? _____

26 What number is midway between 19 and 53? _____

27 Find the area of a square whose perimeter is 12 cm. _____

Using this world time chart answer the following.

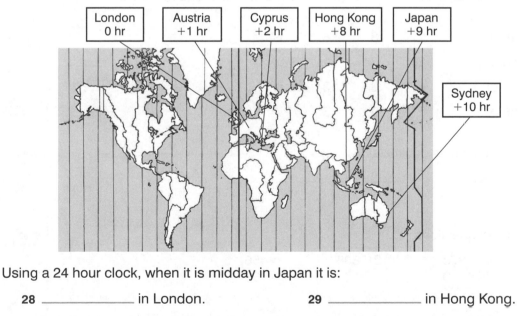

Using a 24 hour clock, when it is midday in Japan it is:

28 _____ in London.   **29** _____ in Hong Kong.

30 It is 12:00 midday in Cyprus. Using a 24 hour clock, what time is it in Austria? _____

31 It is 4:36 p.m. in Hong Kong. What time is it in London? _____

A fair coin is tossed at the start of a game. Underline the correct answer to each question.

32 What is the probability of getting a head?

$\frac{2}{3}$ $\frac{4}{5}$ $\frac{1}{2}$ $\frac{3}{4}$

33 What is the probability of getting a tail?

$\frac{2}{3}$ $\frac{4}{5}$ $\frac{1}{2}$ $\frac{3}{4}$

Which numbers are the arrows pointing to on this number line?

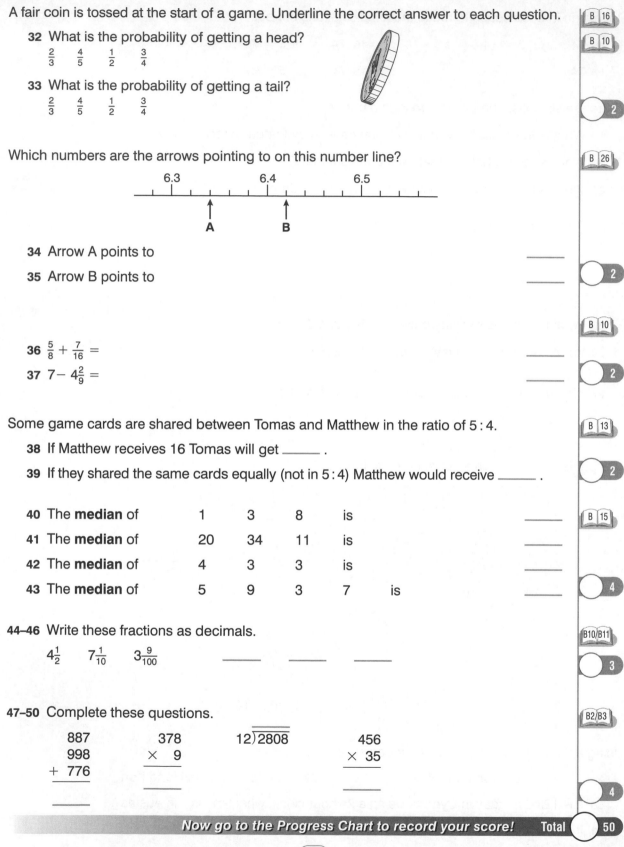

34 Arrow A points to   _____

35 Arrow B points to   _____

36 $\frac{5}{8} + \frac{7}{16} =$ _____

37 $7 - 4\frac{2}{9} =$ _____

Some game cards are shared between Tomas and Matthew in the ratio of 5 : 4.

38 If Matthew receives 16 Tomas will get _____ .

39 If they shared the same cards equally (not in 5 : 4) Matthew would receive _____ .

40 The **median** of   1   3   8   is   _____

41 The **median** of   20   34   11   is   _____

42 The **median** of   4   3   3   is   _____

43 The **median** of   5   9   3   7   is   _____

44–46 Write these fractions as decimals.

$4\frac{1}{2}$ $7\frac{1}{10}$ $3\frac{9}{100}$ _____   _____   _____

47–50 Complete these questions.

$$
\begin{array}{r}
887 \\
998 \\
+\ 776 \\
\hline
\end{array}
\qquad
\begin{array}{r}
378 \\
\times\ 9 \\
\hline
\end{array}
\qquad
12\overline{)2808}
\qquad
\begin{array}{r}
456 \\
\times\ 35 \\
\hline
\end{array}
$$

Now go to the Progress Chart to record your score!   Total   50

B 16
B 10
2
B 26
2
B 10
2
B 13
2
B 15
4
B10/B11
3
B2/B3
4

Paper 3

1 Which of the numbers in the oval is 2^2? _____

2 Which of the numbers in the oval is 5^2? _____

3 Which of the numbers in the oval is 3^2 _____

4 Which of the numbers in the oval is 6^2 _____

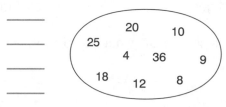

4

5–15 Complete this timetable for Merrywell School. There are five lessons each 35 minutes in length, with a break of 15 minutes after the third lesson.

	Begins	**Ends**
1st lesson	_____	_____
2nd lesson	_____	_____
3rd lesson	_____	_____
Break	_____	1:10
4th lesson	_____	_____
5th lesson	_____	_____

11

16 What is the nearest number to 1000, but smaller than 1000, into which 38 will divide with no remainder? _____

1

What is the area of:

17 side A? _____   18 side B? _____

19 side C? _____

What is the perimeter of:

20 side A? _____   21 side B? _____

22 side C? _____

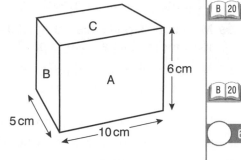

6

Which number is represented by each symbol?

23 $2 \times \triangle = 4 \times 5$ $\triangle =$ _____

24 $5 \times \clubsuit = 27 - 2$ $\clubsuit =$ _____

25 $\otimes \times 3 = 36 \div 3$ $\otimes =$ _____

26 $\blacklozenge \times 4 = 10 + 10$ $\blacklozenge =$ _____

4

Chris is 11 years old and Emma is 9.

They are given £40 to be shared between them in the ratio of their ages.

B 13
2

27 Chris will get _____   **28** Emma will get _____

29 If 11 items cost £7.37, what would be the cost of 8 items?   _____

B4/B3
1

Find the area of these triangles.

B 18

Scale: 1 square = 1 cm²

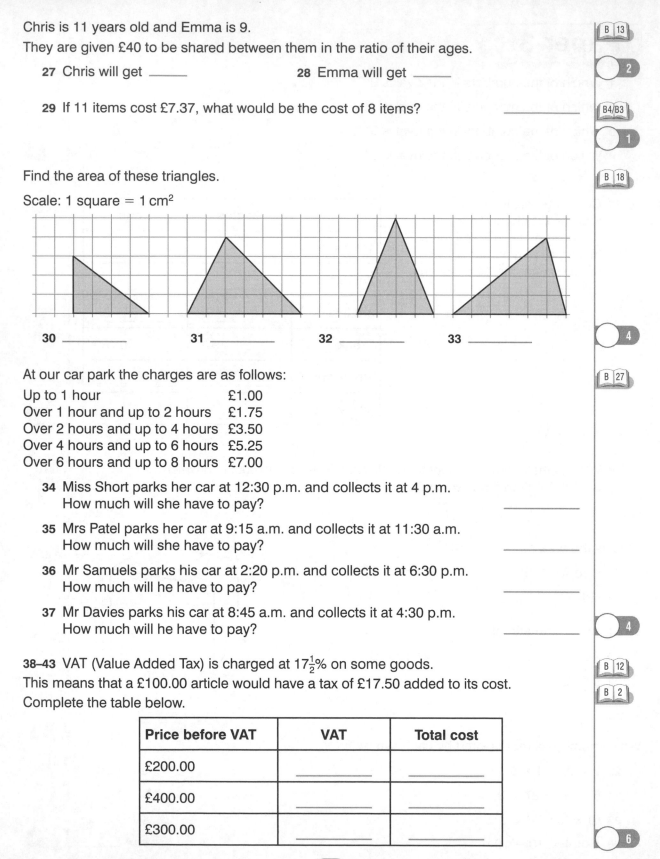

30 _____   **31** _____   **32** _____   **33** _____

4

At our car park the charges are as follows:

B 27

Up to 1 hour	£1.00
Over 1 hour and up to 2 hours	£1.75
Over 2 hours and up to 4 hours	£3.50
Over 4 hours and up to 6 hours	£5.25
Over 6 hours and up to 8 hours	£7.00

34 Miss Short parks her car at 12:30 p.m. and collects it at 4 p.m.
How much will she have to pay?   _____

35 Mrs Patel parks her car at 9:15 a.m. and collects it at 11:30 a.m.
How much will she have to pay?   _____

36 Mr Samuels parks his car at 2:20 p.m. and collects it at 6:30 p.m.
How much will he have to pay?   _____

37 Mr Davies parks his car at 8:45 a.m. and collects it at 4:30 p.m.
How much will he have to pay?   _____

4

38–43 VAT (Value Added Tax) is charged at $17\frac{1}{2}$% on some goods.
This means that a £100.00 article would have a tax of £17.50 added to its cost.
Complete the table below.

B 12
B 2

Price before VAT	VAT	Total cost
£200.00	_____	_____
£400.00	_____	_____
£300.00	_____	_____

6

44	m	cm		45	m	cm		46	m	cm
	4	72			6	2			4	60
+ 3	39			− 3	8			×		5

47–50 Write these numbers to the nearest 100.

    298   847   503   1074

_____   _____   _____   _____

Now go to the Progress Chart to record your score!   **Total**   50

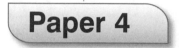

Paper 4

1–5 Fill in the gaps.

	Length	Width	Perimeter
Rectangle 1	18 cm	_____	40 cm
Rectangle 2	_____	3 cm	30 cm
Rectangle 3	9 cm	4 cm	_____
Square	6 cm	_____	_____

6 How many times can 28 be subtracted from 1316?   _____

7–12 Circle the correct answer in each line.

0.1 × 0.1	=	0.2	0.02	0.01	0.1	1.1
10% of 40	=	8	5	80	20	4
10 − 9.99	=	0.9	0.01	1.00	1.1	1.9
0.207 ÷ 0.3	=	0.9	0.09	0.69	0.66	0.23
1.1 × 1.1	=	1.21	1.11	11.1	2.2	1.01
567 ÷ 100	=	56 700	0.567	56.7	5.67	5670

13 The product of two numbers is 1260. One of the numbers is 35. What is the other number?   _____

14–20 Write the missing digits or answer.

$$\begin{array}{r} 3\,6\,5 \\ 2\,\_\,\_\,1 \\ +\ 3\,4\,5\,\_ \\ \hline 1\,0\,6\,0\,3 \end{array}$$

$$\begin{array}{r} 1\,\_\,7\,\_ \\ -\ \ 2\,\_\,5 \\ \hline 7\,8\,6 \end{array}$$

$$\begin{array}{r} 3\,4\,5 \\ \times\ \ \_\,\_ \\ \hline 2\,4\,1\,5 \end{array}$$

$$9)\,\overline{\ \ 3\,8\ \ }$$

Find the value of y in the following equations.

21 $3y = 10 - 1$

$y =$ _____

22 $4y - y = 12$

$y =$ _____

23 $2y + y = 6$

$y =$ _____

24 $3y + y = 11 + 1$

$y =$ _____

Which numbers are the arrows pointing to on this number line?

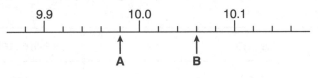

25 Arrow A points to _____

26 Arrow B points to _____

A fair dice numbered 1 to 6 is rolled at the start of a game. Underline the correct answer to each question.

27 What is the probability of getting a 6?

$\frac{2}{3}$ $\frac{1}{6}$ $\frac{1}{2}$ $\frac{3}{4}$

28 What is the probability of getting a 5?

$\frac{1}{3}$ $\frac{1}{4}$ $\frac{1}{5}$ $\frac{1}{6}$

29 What is the probability of getting a 2 or a 3?

$\frac{1}{6}$ $\frac{1}{3}$ $\frac{1}{2}$ $\frac{2}{3}$

What are the missing numbers in these number squares?

38	34	30
42	38	34
x	42	38

102	120	y
84	102	120
66	84	102

z	27	31
27	31	35
31	35	39

30 $x =$ _____   **31** $y =$ _____   **32** $z =$ _____

B2/B3

7

B8/B2

B 3

4

B 26

2

B 16

3

B 7

3

Multiply each of these numbers by 10.

33 3.77 _____   **34** 46.5 _____

35 0.126 _____   **36** 0.027 _____

37 49 _____   **38** 567 _____

39 0.0023 _____

B 1
7

Find the **median** of the following sets of numbers.

40   4   6   8   10   _____

41   8   2   6   8   _____

42   54   21   7   19   _____

43   1   2   3   4   5   6   _____

44   32   21   60   3   5   17   _____

45   45   47   _____

B 15
6

Change these 24-hour times into 12-hour times using a.m. or p.m.

46 05:05 _____   **47** 12:45 _____   **48** 20:02 _____

49 15:15 _____   **50** 11:14 _____

B 27
5

Now go to the Progress Chart to record your score!   Total (50)

Paper 5

1–7 Complete the following chart.

B 20

	Length	**Width**	**Area**
Rectangle 1	8 m	6 m	_____
Rectangle 2	_____	4 m	32 m²
Rectangle 3	4 m	_____	10 m²
Rectangle 4	_____	3.5 m	10.5 m²
Rectangle 5	1.5 m	1.5 m	_____
Rectangle 6	5 m	_____	6 m²
Rectangle 7	1.3 m	2 m	_____

7

Find the area of these triangles.

Scale: 1 square = 1 cm²

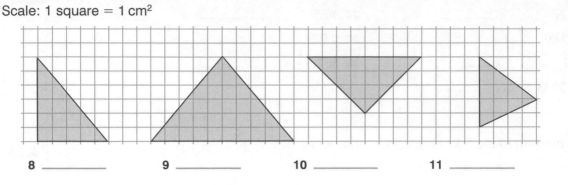

8 _____   9 _____   10 _____   11 _____

12 My watch loses a quarter of a minute every hour. If I put it right at midday, what time will my watch show at 8 p.m. that evening?   _____

A class carried out a survey to find the most popular subject.

Favourite subject	Votes
English	5
Mathematics	12
PE	7
Music	6

13 Which is the most popular subject?   _____

14 Which is the least popular subject?   _____

15 How many votes are there in total?   ____

16 What is the **mean** number of votes?   ____

17–22 Complete the table.

▽	2	4	6	8	10	12
2 × ▽ =						

Reduce these prices by 10%.

23 £50   _____   **24** £110   _____

25 £250   _____   **26** £40   _____

27 £30   _____   **28** £280   _____

29–30 One day 20% of the children were away from school on a visit to a museum.

If there were 360 children altogether, _____ children were in school and _____ were on the museum trip.

B 12
2

31 A number multiplied by itself is 16. What is the number? _____

B 6
1

32 How many US Dollars do you get for £10? _____

33 How many Kenyan Shillings do you get for £100? _____

34 How many Euros do you get for £1000? _____

| £1 = 1.46 US Dollars |
| £1 = 119 Kenyan Shillings |
| £1 = 1.42 Euros |

B 3
B 13
3

A bag contains 4 grey balls and 3 white balls. Underline the correct answer to each question.

35 What is the probability of picking a white ball?

$\frac{3}{4}$ $\frac{3}{5}$ $\frac{3}{6}$ $\frac{3}{7}$ $\frac{3}{8}$

36 What is the probability of picking a grey ball?

0 $\frac{1}{2}$ $\frac{4}{7}$ $\frac{3}{7}$ $\frac{3}{4}$

37 What is the probability of picking a black ball?

0 $\frac{1}{2}$ $\frac{4}{7}$ $\frac{3}{7}$ $\frac{3}{4}$

B 16
3

38 What number when divided by 12, has an answer 11 remainder 5? _____

B 3
1

A concert starts at 7:30 p.m. The first half of the programme lasts 1 hour 35 minutes, then there is an interval of 8 minutes.

39 When does the second half of the concert begin? _____ p.m.

B 27
1

A rectangular field is 3 times as long as it is wide. If the perimeter is 0.8 km:

40 what is the length? _____

41 what is the width? _____

42 what is the area? _____

B 20
3

43 I have enough tinned dog food to last my 2 dogs for 18 days. If I got another dog, how long would this food last? _____ B4/B3

44 Add the greatest number to the smallest number.

565   656   556   655   566   665   _____ B 2

45 What number is halfway between 37 and 111? _____ B 2

46–47 Put a circle around the **prime numbers**. B 5

12   13   14   15   16   17   18

48–50 What are the **prime factors** of 60? _____ and _____ and _____ B 6

8

Now go to the Progress Chart to record your score!   Total   50

Paper 6

1–3 Write down the numbers that will come out of this machine. B 9

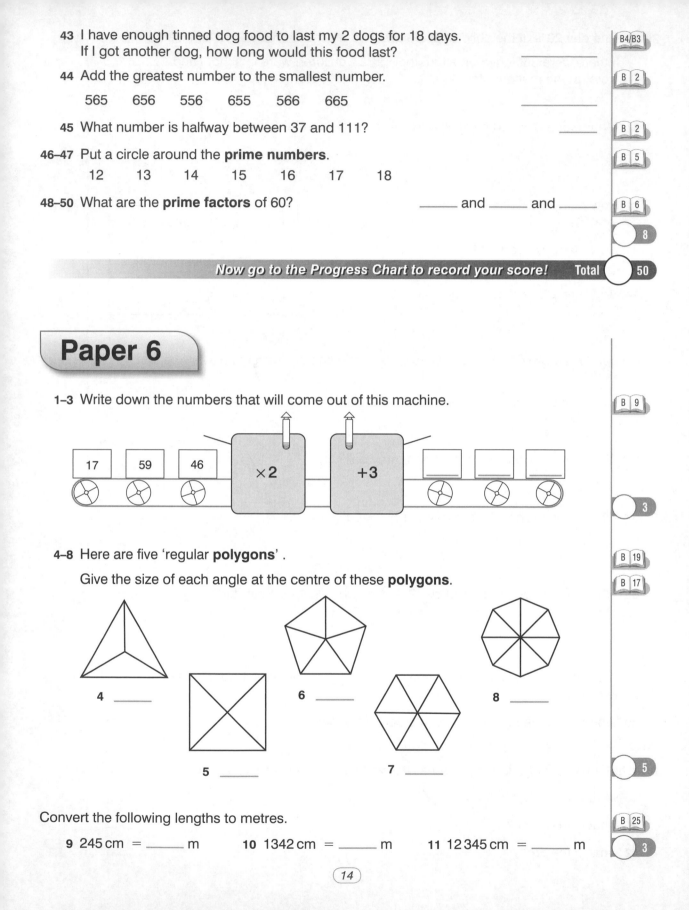

3

4–8 Here are five 'regular **polygons**' . B 19

Give the size of each angle at the centre of these **polygons**. B 17

4 _____

5 _____

6 _____

7 _____

8 _____

5

Convert the following lengths to metres. B 25

9 245 cm = _____ m   **10** 1342 cm = _____ m   **11** 12 345 cm = _____ m 3

Convert the following lengths to kilometres.

12 1357 m = _____ km

13 12 986 m = _____ km

14 456 m = _____ km

15–16 There are 30 children in Class 4. 60% of them are girls.

There are _____ girls and _____ boys.

17 Which number, when multiplied by 30, will give the same answer as 51 × 10?   _____

18 Write the number which is 7 less than 2000.   _____

19–34 Insert a sign in each space so that the answer given for each line and column is correct.

3		3		2	=	7
	■		■		■	
6		4		5	=	5
	■		■		■	
2		5		4	=	6
=	■	=	■	=	■	=
9		2		6	=	12

35 If 9 items cost £6.30, what will be the cost of 11 items?   _____

Here is a list of some of the longest rivers in the world.

Write the length of each river to the nearest 1000 km.

36 Amazon	6516 km	_____ km
37 Chang Jiang	6380 km	_____ km
38 Nile	6695 km	_____ km
39 Paraná	4500 km	_____ km
40 Mississippi−Missouri	6019 km	_____ km
41 Zaire	4667 km	_____ km

15

Fill in the spaces with one of these signs.   < > =

42 8×9 _____ 6×12

43 $8 + 9 + 7$ _____ $30 - 3$

44 0.5 m _____ 45 cm

45 23 _____ 3^2

46 12^2 _____ 144

47 50 min _____ $\frac{3}{4}$ hour

Consider a fair dice with faces numbered 1 to 6.

What is the probability of rolling:

48 a 4 or a 5? _____   **49** a 7? _____

50 a whole number greater than 0 and less than 7? _____

Now go to the Progress Chart to record your score! **Total** 50

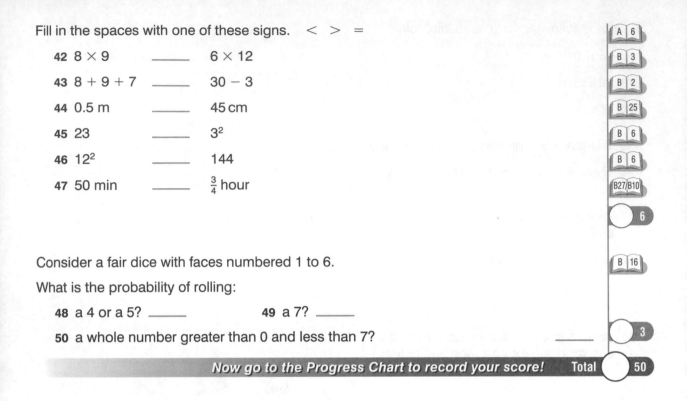

Paper 7

Underline the correct answer in each line.

1 0.2×0.2 = 0.4   4   40   0.04   0.004

2 $\frac{1}{2} + \frac{1}{4}$ = $\frac{2}{6}$ $\frac{3}{4}$ $\frac{2}{4}$ $\frac{2}{8}$ $\frac{1}{8}$

3 50% of 30 = 35   20   25   130   15

4 $10 \div \frac{1}{2}$ = 20   5 $10\frac{1}{2}$ $\frac{1}{20}$ $\frac{1}{5}$

5 $5 \div 0.5$ = 0.1   0.01   100   10   0.001

6 $412 \div 4$ = 13   103   104   12   14

7 $\frac{1}{8} + \frac{1}{2}$ = $\frac{1}{16}$ $\frac{1}{10}$ $\frac{5}{8}$ $\frac{1}{2}$ $\frac{3}{8}$

Three buses leave the bus station at 7 a.m. Service A runs every 5 minutes. Service B runs every 15 minutes. Service C runs every 12 minutes.

8 At what time will all three services again start from the bus station at the same time? _____

Here is a list of some of the highest mountains in the world.
Write the height of each mountain to the nearest 1000 feet.

B 1

9 Aconcagua   22 834 feet   _____ feet

10 Everest   29 028 feet   _____ feet

11 K2   28 250 feet   _____ feet

12 Kilimanjaro   19 340 feet   _____ feet

13 McKinley   20 320 feet   _____ feet

14 Mont Blanc   15 744 feet   _____ feet

6

15 What number, when multiplied by 10, has the same answer as 15×12? _____

B 3

1

16–18 Andrew has half as many computer games as Stuart, who has half as many as Meena. Together they have 140 computer games.

Meena has _____ computer games, Stuart has _____ and Andrew has _____ .

B 13

3

Here is the attendance record of 40 children for one week of the term.

B 15

Attendance	Mon	Tues	Wed	Thurs	Fri
Morning	36	33	37	34	35
Afternoon	39	36	38	36	36

19 What was the **mean** (average) morning attendance? _____

20 What was the **median** afternoon attendance? _____

21 What was the **mode** afternoon attendance? _____

3

Multiply each of these numbers by 1000.

B 1

22 37.8 _____   23 2.45 _____

24 0.047 _____   25 25.0 _____

26 0.82 _____

5

27 $7\frac{7}{8} + 5\frac{13}{16} =$ _____

28 $7\frac{1}{5} - 3\frac{11}{15} =$ _____

B 10

2

29 What is the total area of the flag? _____

30 What is the area of the cross? _____

31 What is the area of the grey area? _____

32 What is the perimeter of the flag? _____

33 What is the perimeter of the cross? _____

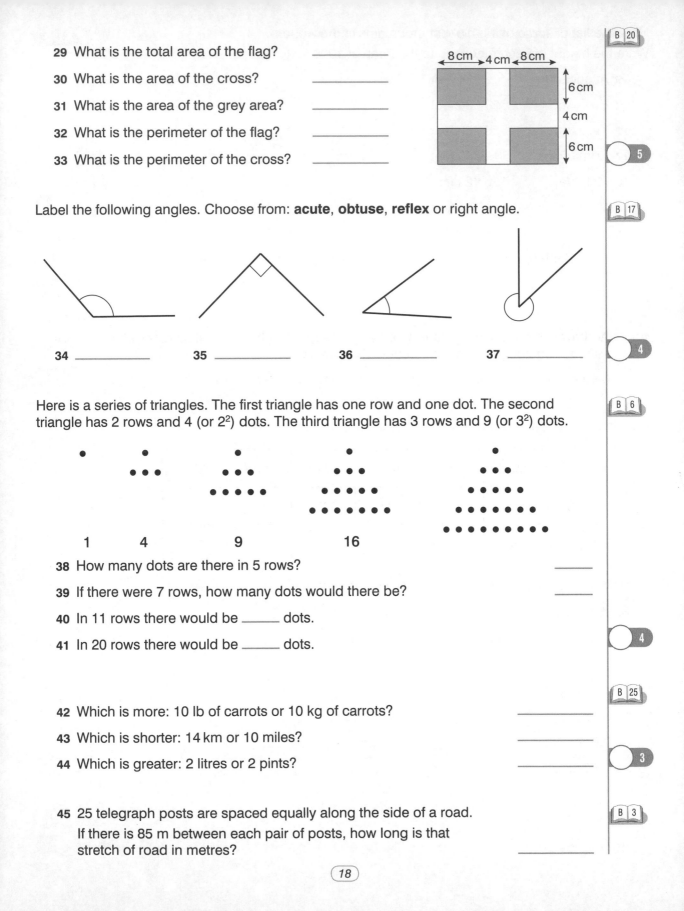

Label the following angles. Choose from: **acute**, **obtuse**, **reflex** or right angle.

34 _____ **35** _____ **36** _____ **37** _____

Here is a series of triangles. The first triangle has one row and one dot. The second triangle has 2 rows and 4 (or 2^2) dots. The third triangle has 3 rows and 9 (or 3^2) dots.

1   4   9   16

38 How many dots are there in 5 rows? _____

39 If there were 7 rows, how many dots would there be? _____

40 In 11 rows there would be _____ dots.

41 In 20 rows there would be _____ dots.

42 Which is more: 10 lb of carrots or 10 kg of carrots? _____

43 Which is shorter: 14 km or 10 miles? _____

44 Which is greater: 2 litres or 2 pints? _____

45 25 telegraph posts are spaced equally along the side of a road. If there is 85 m between each pair of posts, how long is that stretch of road in metres? _____

46 A man's salary was £16 000. He is given a 5% increase.
What is his new salary? _____ B12/B2

47 A cricketer's average score for 6 innings is 12 runs.
What must he score in his next innings to make his average 13? _____ B4/B15

B 2

48 Add together 4.5 m, 16.7 m and 127.09 m. _____ B 2

4

49–50 Complete the drawings below using the line of symmetry marked by the dashes. B 24

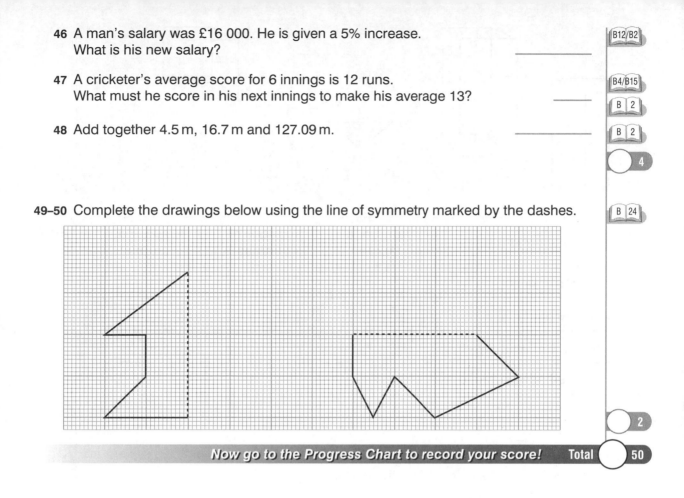

2

Now go to the Progress Chart to record your score!   Total   50

Paper 8

1 What is the difference between 0.225 tonnes and 128 kg? _____ kg   B25/B2

2 If $a = 2$ and $b = 3$, find the value of $4a - 2b$. _____ B 8

3 A book has 38 lines to each page.
On which page will the 1000th line appear? _____ B 3

3

Change these 12-hour times into 24-hour times. B 27

4 10:10 a.m. _____

5 11:20 p.m. _____

6 1:01 a.m. _____

7 7:45 p.m. _____

4

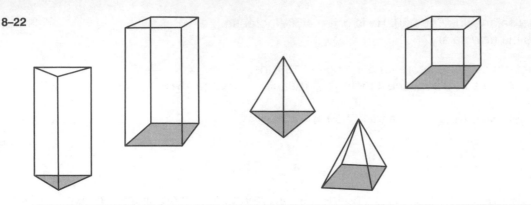

Name of solid	Number of faces	Number of vertices	Number of edges
Triangular prism			
Square prism			
Triangular-based pyramid			
Square-based pyramid			
Cube			

B 21

15

23 Mrs Forgetmenot is 9 minutes late for the 9.42 a.m. train.
How long will she have to wait for the train at 10.27 a.m.? _____

B 27

1

24–28 Local clubs took part in a 'clean the beach' campaign. Work out the percentage of members from each club that took part in this activity.

B 12

Club	Number of members	Number who took part	Percentage
A	100	79	_____
B	50	36	_____
C	150	120	_____
D	70	49	_____
E	80	60	_____

5

29 If $x = 5$ and $y = 2$ then $\dfrac{4x}{5y} =$ _____

B 8

1

30–40 Complete the timetable for Workmore School. There are five lessons, each 30 minutes long, with a break of 15 minutes after the third lesson.

	Begins	**Ends**
1st lesson	_____	_____
2nd lesson	_____	_____
3rd lesson	_____	_____
Break	_____	_____
4th lesson	_____	_____
5th lesson	_____	12:25

11

41 Three whole numbers multiplied together total 2475. Two of the numbers are 25 and 11. What is the third number? _____

42–43 5 is a **prime factor** of 2475.
What are the other two prime factors? _____ and _____

3

£1 = 1.46 US Dollars	£1 = 118 Kenyan Shillings
£1 = 1.42 Euros	£1 = 2.13 Australian Dollars

44 How many US Dollars do you get for £3? _____ US Dollars

45 How many Kenyan Shillings do you get for £1.50? _____ Kenyan Shillings

46 How many Euros do you get for £13? _____ Euros

47 How many Australian Dollars do you get for £50? _____ Australian Dollars

4

There are 351 children in a school. There are 7 boys to every 6 girls.

48 How many boys are there? _____

49 How many girls are there? _____

2

A number multiplied by itself and then doubled is 242.

50 What is the number? _____

1

Now go to the Progress Chart to record your score! Total 50

Paper 9

Use these words to help you name the following shapes:
rhombus, **kite**, **parallelogram**, **trapezium**, rectangle.

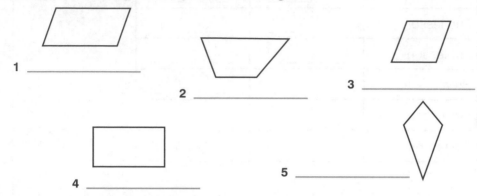

1 _____

2 _____

3 _____

4 _____

5 _____

B 19

On one day in February the temperatures in different places were:

Chicago	−3 °C	Montreal	−10 °C	Singapore	31 °C
Cape Town	27 °C	Miami	26 °C	Toronto	−5 °C

B6/B2

6 Which was the hottest of these places? _____

7 Which was the coldest? _____

8 How much colder was it in Chicago than Cape Town? _____

9 The difference between Toronto and Miami was _____

10 The difference between Singapore and Montreal was _____

11 Form the largest number possible with the digits 3, 9, 7 and 2 and then take away the smallest possible number. What is your answer? _____

B1/B2

12 How many comics, costing 70p each, can be bought for £15.00? _____

B 3

13 In a certain question Mia multiplied by 7 instead of dividing by 7. Her answer was 6027. What should it have been?

B 3

$y \times 7 = 6027$ ✗ $y \div 7 = $ _____ ✓

Write the next two numbers in each line.

B 7

14–15	$3\frac{1}{2}$	$4\frac{1}{4}$	5	$5\frac{3}{4}$	_____	_____
16–17	100	90	81	73	_____	_____
18–19	47	52	58	65	_____	_____
20–21	2	5	11	20	_____	_____
22–23	2	4	8	16	_____	_____

24–25 The perimeter of a rectangular piece of paper is 48 cm.
The length is 3 times the width. The length is _____ and the width is _____

26–30

You start facing	turn through	clockwise/ anticlockwise	you are now facing
W	135°	anticlockwise	_____
SE	45°	clockwise	_____
NE	90°	anticlockwise	_____
SW	45°	anticlockwise	_____
S	180°	clockwise	_____

3 pencils and 4 ballpoint pens cost £1.70.

3 pencils and 2 ballpoint pens cost £1.30.

Use this information to find the cost of:

31 2 ballpoint pens _____   **32** 1 ballpoint pen _____

33 3 pencils _____   **34** 1 pencil _____

Divide each of the following numbers by 1000.

35 385 _____   **36** 0.12 _____

37 7.8 _____   **38** 49 _____

The population of Grangetown is 11 552. The men and children together number 8763, and the men and women number 5874.

39 How many women are there? _____

40 There are _____ children.

41 How many men are there? _____

Find the following:

42 The **factors** of 12 are 1, 2, _____, _____, _____ and _____ .

43 The **factors** of 20 are 1, _____, _____, _____, _____ and _____ .

44 The **factors** of 15 are _____, _____, _____ and _____ .

45 The numbers that are **factors** of both 12 and 20 are 1, _____ and _____ .

46 The numbers that are **factors** of both 12 and 15 are 1 and _____ .

47 The numbers that are **factors** of both 20 and 15 are 1 and _____ .

48–50 Now fill in the lengths of the sides of the box using these answers.

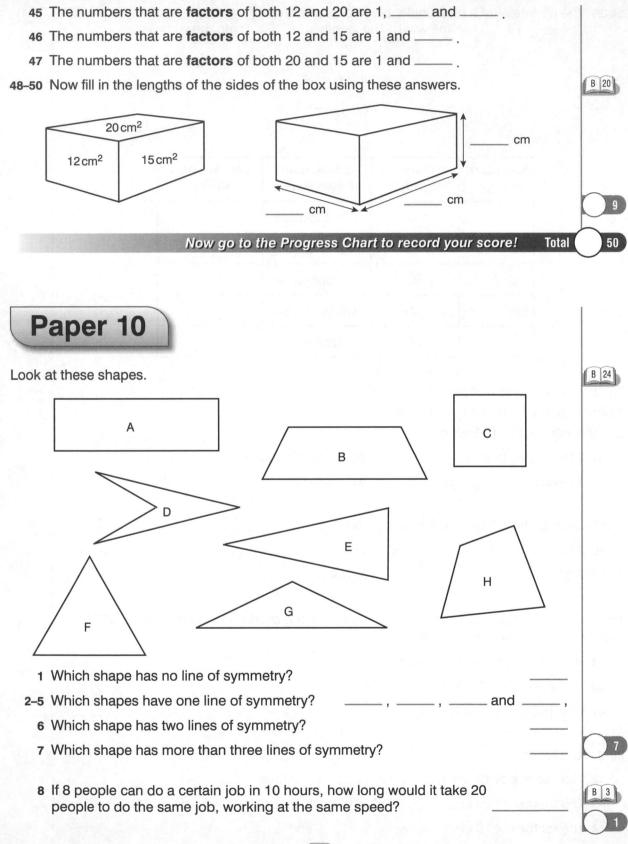

Now go to the Progress Chart to record your score! Total 50

Paper 10

Look at these shapes.

1 Which shape has no line of symmetry? _____

2–5 Which shapes have one line of symmetry? _____ , _____ , _____ and _____ ,

6 Which shape has two lines of symmetry? _____

7 Which shape has more than three lines of symmetry? _____

8 If 8 people can do a certain job in 10 hours, how long would it take 20 people to do the same job, working at the same speed? _____

Find the **mean** of these sets of numbers.

9 7 11 4 6 _____

10 7 1 4 6 2 _____

11 7 11 4 6 2 12 _____

12 Thirty-six posts were spaced evenly along a road that was 1.575 km long.

What was the distance in metres between each pair of posts? _____

13–19 Complete the following chart.

Wholesale price (Price at the factory)	Retail price (Price in the shop)	Profit (Money made by shopkeeper)
£7.85	£9.22	_____
_____	£17.10	£2.34
£38.75	_____	£5.67
£17.37	£21.14	_____
£41.85	_____	£8.19
_____	£67.76	£12.87
£0.87	_____	£0.18

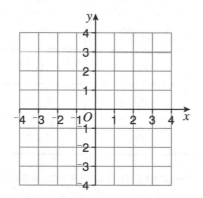

20–24 Plot the following **coordinates** on the chart and join them in the order you plot them.

$(-3, -2)$ $(-3, 3)$ $(-1, 1)$ $(1, 3)$ $(1, -2)$

25 What letter have you made? _____

26–28 Emma (who is 8 years old), Salim (who is 7), and Katie (who is 5), share £10.00 in the ratio of their ages.

Emma gets _____ , Salim gets _____ and Katie gets _____ .

B 13
3
B25/B2

29 What must be added to 375 g to make 1 kg? _____ g

30 How many packets, each holding 125 g, can be filled from a case holding 3 kg? _____

2

Write these numbers as fractions in their **lowest terms**.

B10/B11

31 3.8 _____   **32** 11.4 _____

33 11.002 _____   **34** 3.25 _____

35 6.5 _____   **36** 1.12 _____

6

Mr and Mrs Black took their three children from Norwich to Cromer by train.

The tickets for the five people totalled £31.50.

All the children travelled at half price.

B2/B3
B 4

37 How much was an adult ticket? _____

1
B 27

	Train A	Train B	Train C	Train D
Norwich	06:15	07:33	20:48	22:10
Wroxham	06:26	07:48	20:32	21:54
Worstead	06:35	07:55	20:24	21:47
North Walsham	06:45	08:02	20:19	21:41
Gunton	06:51	08:08	20:09	21:35
Cromer	07:04	08:21	19:57	21:23

38 The fastest train for the Black family going to Cromer was train _____

39 The slowest train for the Black family returning to Norwich was train _____

40 If I leave Wroxham on the 07:48 train, and spend the day in Cromer, leaving on the 19:57 train, how long am I actually in Cromer? _____ h _____ min

41 At what time does the 19:57 train from Cromer arrive in North Walsham? _____

I live in Norwich and travel to Cromer on the 06:15 train, returning home on the 21:23 train.

42 How long will I spend travelling on the train that day? —— h —— min

43 At what time does the 20:09 from Gunton reach Wroxham? _____

⬤ 6

44–46 In a sale all goods were reduced by 20%. Complete the chart below.

B12/B2

Ordinary price	Sale price
£20.00	_____
£35.00	_____
£60.00	_____

⬤ 3

State whether the following statements are TRUE or FALSE.

B 17

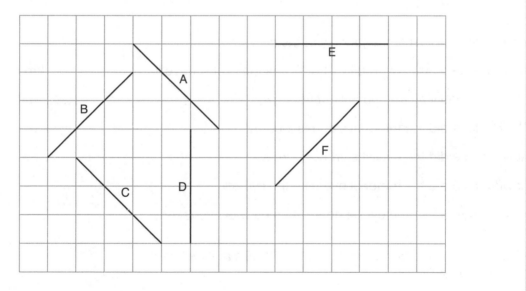

47 Line B is parallel to line A. _____

48 Line C is perpendicular to line F. _____

49 Line E is a horizontal line. _____

50 Line D is a vertical line. _____

⬤ 4

Now go to the Progress Chart to record your score! **Total** ⬤ 50

Paper 11

This graph represents the journeys of a cyclist and a motorist. The motorist is faster than the cyclist.

B 14

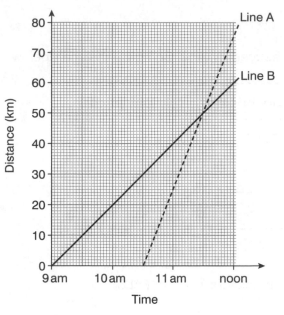

1 Which line represents the journey of the cyclist? _____

2 At what speed (km covered in 1 hour) was the cyclist travelling? _____ km/h

3 At what speed was the motorist travelling? _____ km/h

4 At what time did the motorist start his journey? _____

5 At what time did the cyclist start his journey? _____

6 At what time did the motorist overtake the cyclist? _____

7 How many km had the cyclist done when he was overtaken? _____

8 What would be the approximate cost of 13 CDs at £4.98 each (to the nearest £)? _____

9 The average of 4 numbers is $10\frac{1}{2}$.

If the average of 3 of them is 9, what is the 4th number? _____

10–14 Arrange these fractions in order of size, putting the largest first.

$\frac{1}{2}$ $\qquad$ $\frac{2}{3}$ $\qquad$ $\frac{5}{6}$ $\qquad$ $\frac{3}{8}$ $\qquad$ $\frac{3}{4}$

_____ _____ _____ _____ _____

Some children in a Youth Club made this Venn diagram to show which music they like.

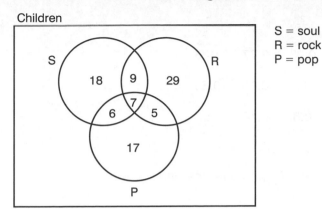

Children

S = soul
R = rock
P = pop

15–17 _____ children like soul, _____ like rock and _____ like pop music.

18 The number of children who like both soul and rock is _____

19 How many like both soul and pop? _____

Here are three shaded cubes.

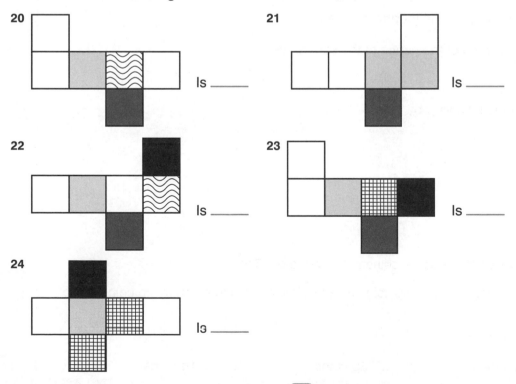

A   B   C

Which cube has the following nets? Choose between A, B, C or none.

20 Is _____

21 Is _____

22 Is _____

23 Is _____

24 Is _____

5

5

Underline the correct answer in each line.

25 $\frac{1}{8} + \frac{1}{4}$ = $\frac{1}{12}$ $\frac{2}{12}$ $\frac{3}{8}$ $\frac{1}{4}$

26 2.00 − 1.77 = 0.33 0.23 3.77 1.23

27 0.3 × 0.3 = 0.09 0.6 0.06 0.33

28 3 ÷ 0.6 = 0.2 0.5 0.18 5

B 10
B 11
4

29–33 Plot the points (1, 3), (1, −1), (−3, −1) on the grid below.

B 23
B 21

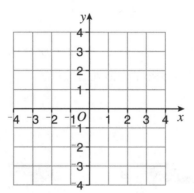

These points are the **vertices** of a square. Mark the fourth **vertex** and draw the square.

34–35 The **coordinates** of the fourth **vertex** are (_____, _____).

36–37 The **coordinates** of the centre of the square are (_____, _____).

9

Multiply each of the following by 100.

B 1

38 26.2 _____

39 8.9 _____

40 25.16 _____

3

41–43 A cash box contains some coins to the value of £5.25.

B 13

There are twice as many 5p coins as 2p coins, and twice as many 2p coins as 1p coins.

This means there are:

_____ 5p coins _____ 2p coins _____ 1p coins

3

Any answer that requires units of measurement should be marked wrong if the correct units have not been included.

Paper 1

1. 15
2. 30
3. 30
4. 15
5. 30
6. 6
7. 4
8. 4
9. 9990
10. $\frac{1}{2}$ (smallest)
11. $\frac{7}{8}$ (largest)
12. 0.307 (smallest)
13. 37 (largest)
14. $\frac{10}{10}$ (smallest)
15. $\frac{15}{3}$ (largest)
16. 0.125 (smallest)
17. $\frac{7}{8}$ (largest)
18. $\frac{2}{5}$ of 10 (smallest)
19. $\frac{5}{7}$ of 14 (largest)
20. 102 021
21. 169
22. 209
23. 389
24. 449
25. 60°
26. 150°
27. 120°
28. NOT gloss washable paint
29. Is it gloss?
30. 5
31. 2
32. 3
33. 5

34–37

38. (−1, −2)
39. 21:45
40. 10:50
41. 12:55
42. 4
43. 12
44. 20
45. +
46. ÷
47. ×
48. ÷
49. 24
50. 28

Paper 2

1. 7.865
2. 0.654
3. 46.75
4. 0.0123
5. 49
6. 47
7. 45
8. 43
9. 185
10. 222
11. 40
12. 80
13. 60 miles
14. 50 miles
15. ÷
16. +
17. −
18. ×
19. $\frac{1}{2}$ or $\frac{3}{6}$
20. $\frac{1}{6}$
21. $\frac{1}{2}$ or $\frac{3}{6}$
22. 3
23. 5
24. 7
25. 30
26. 36
27. 9 cm²
28. 03:00
29. 11:00
30. 11:00
31. 8:36 a.m.
32. $\frac{1}{2}$
33. $\frac{1}{2}$
34. 6.34
35. 6.42
36. $\frac{17}{16}$ or $1\frac{1}{16}$
37. $2\frac{7}{9}$ or $\frac{25}{9}$
38. 20
39. 18
40. 3
41. 20
42. 3
43. 6
44. 4.5
45. 7.1
46. 3.09
47. 2661
48. 3402
49. 234
50. 15 960

Paper 3

1. 4
2. 25
3. 9
4. 36

5–15

	Begins	Ends
1st lesson	11:10	11:45
2nd lesson	11:45	12:20
3rd lesson	12:20	12:55
Break	12:55	1:10
4th lesson	1:10	1:45
5th lesson	1:45	2:20

16. 988
17. 60 cm²
18. 30 cm²
19. 50 cm²
20. 32 cm
21. 22 cm
22. 30 cm
23. 10
24. 5
25. 4
26. 5
27. £22
28. £18
29. £5.36
30. 6 cm²
31. 12 cm²
32. 10 cm²
33. 12 cm²
34. £3.50
35. £3.50
36. £5.25
37. £7.00

38–43

Price before VAT	VAT	Total cost
£200.00	£35.00	£235.00
£400.00	£70.00	£470.00
£300.00	£52.50	£352.50

44. 8 m 11 cm
45. 2 m 94 cm
46. 23 m
47. 300
48. 800
49. 500
50. 1100

Paper 4

1. 2 cm
2. 12 cm
3. 26 cm
4. 6 cm
5. 24 cm
6. 47
7. 0.01
8. 4
9. 0.01
10. 0.69

11 1.21
12 5.67
13 36
14 4365
15 2781
16 3457
17 1071
18 285
19 7
20 342
21 3
22 4
23 2
24 3
25 9.98
26 10.06
27 $\frac{1}{6}$
28 $\frac{1}{6}$
29 $\frac{1}{3}$
30 46
31 138
32 23
33 37.7
34 465
35 1.26
36 0.27
37 490
38 5670
39 0.023
40 7
41 7
42 20
43 3.5
44 19
45 46
46 5:05 a.m.
47 12:45 p.m.
48 8:02 p.m.
49 3:15 p.m.
50 11:14 a.m.

Paper 5

1–7

	Length	Width	Area
Rectangle 1	8 m	6 m	**48 m²**
Rectangle 2	**8 m**	4 m	32 m²
Rectangle 3	4 m	**2.5 m**	10 m²
Rectangle 4	**3 m**	3.5 m	10.5 m²
Rectangle 5	1.5 m	1.5 m	**2.25 m²**
Rectangle 6	5 m	**1.2 m**	6 m²
Rectangle 7	1.3 m	2 m	**2.6 m²**

8 15 cm²
9 30 cm²
10 16 cm²
11 10 cm²
12 7:58 p.m.
13 Mathematics
14 English
15 30
16 7.5 or $7\frac{1}{2}$

17–22

▽	2	4	6	8	10	12
2 × ▽ =	**4**	**8**	**12**	**16**	**20**	**24**

23 £45
24 £99
25 £225
26 £36
27 £27
28 £252
29 288
30 72
31 4
32 14.6
33 11 900
34 1420
35 $\frac{3}{7}$
36 $\frac{4}{7}$
37 0
38 137
39 9:13 p.m.
40 0.3 km or 300 m
41 0.1 km or 100 m
42 0.03 km² or 30 000 m²
43 12 days
44 1221
45 74
46–47 13, 17
48–50 2, 3, 5

Paper 6

1 37
2 121
3 95
4 120°
5 90°
6 72°
7 60°
8 45°
9 2.45
10 13.42
11 123.45
12 1.357
13 12.986
14 0.456
15 18

16 12
17 17
18 1993

19–34

3	×	3	−	2	=	7
×		+		×		−
6	+	4	−	5	=	5
÷		−		−		×
2	×	5	−	4	=	6
=		=		=		=
9	×	2	−	6	=	12

35 £7.70
36 7000
37 6000
38 7000
39 5000
40 6000
41 5000
42 =
43 <
44 >
45 >
46 =
47 >
48 $\frac{2}{6}$ or $\frac{1}{3}$
49 0
50 1 or $\frac{6}{6}$

Paper 7

1 0.04
2 $\frac{3}{4}$
3 15
4 20
5 10
6 103
7 $\frac{5}{8}$
8 8 a.m.
9 23 000
10 29 000
11 28 000
12 19 000
13 20 000
14 16 000
15 18
16 80
17 40
18 20
19 35
20 36
21 36
22 37 800
23 2450
24 47
25 25 000

26 820

27 $\frac{219}{16}$ or $13\frac{11}{16}$

28 $\frac{52}{15}$ or $3\frac{7}{15}$

29 320 cm²

30 128 cm²

31 192 cm²

32 72 cm

33 72 cm

34 obtuse

35 right angle

36 acute

37 reflex

38 25

39 49

40 121

41 400

42 10 kg

43 14 km

44 2 litres

45 2040 m

46 £16 800

47 19

48 148.29 m

49–50

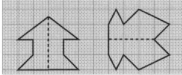

24–28

Club	Number of members	Number who took part	Percentage
A	100	79	**79**
B	50	36	**72**
C	150	120	**80**
D	70	49	**70**
E	80	60	**75**

29 2

30–40

	Begins	Ends
1st lesson	**09:40**	**10:10**
2nd lesson	**10:10**	**10:40**
3rd lesson	**10:40**	**11:10**
Break	**11:10**	**11:25**
4th lesson	**11:25**	**11:55**
5th lesson	**11:55**	12:25

41 9

42–43 3, 11

44 4.38

45 177

46 18.46

47 106.5

48 189

49 162

50 11

Paper 8

1 97

2 2

3 27

4 10:10

5 23:20

6 01:01

7 19:45

8–22

Name of solid	Faces	Vertices	Edges
Triangular prism	5	6	9
Square prism	6	8	12
Triangular-based pyramid	4	4	6
Square-based pyramid	5	5	8
Cube	6	8	12

23 36 min

Paper 9

1 parallelogram

2 trapezium

3 rhombus

4 rectangle

5 kite

6 Singapore

7 Montreal

8 30°C

9 31°C

10 41°C

11 7353

12 21

13 123

14–15 $6\frac{1}{2}$, $7\frac{1}{4}$

16–17 66, 60

18–19 73, 82

20–21 32, 47

22–23 32, 64

24 18 cm

25 6 cm

26 SE

27 S

28 NW

29 S

30 N

31 40p

32 20p

33 90p

34 30p

35 0.385

36 0.000 12

37 0.0078

38 0.049

39 2789

40 5678

41 3085

42 3, 4, 6, 12

43 2, 4, 5, 10, 20

44 1, 3, 5, 15

45 2, 4

46 3

47 5

48–50

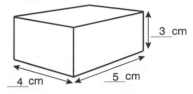

Paper 10

1 H

2–5 B, D, E, G

6 A

7 C

8 4 hours

9 7

10 4

11 7

12 45 m

13–19

Wholesale price	Retail price	Profit
£7.85	£9.22	**£1.37**
£14.76	£17.10	£2.34
£38.75	**£44.42**	£5.67
£17.37	£21.14	**£3.77**
£41.85	**£50.04**	£8.19
£54.89	£67.76	£12.87
£0.87	**£1.05**	£0.18

20–24

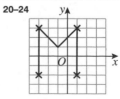

25 M
26 £4.00
27 £3.50
28 £2.50
29 625
30 24
31 $\frac{19}{5}$ or $3\frac{4}{5}$
32 $\frac{57}{5}$ or $11\frac{2}{5}$
33 $\frac{5501}{500}$ or $11\frac{1}{500}$
34 $\frac{13}{4}$ or $3\frac{1}{4}$
35 $\frac{13}{2}$ or $6\frac{1}{2}$
36 $\frac{28}{25}$ or $1\frac{3}{25}$
37 £9
38 B
39 C
40 11 h 36 min
41 20:19
42 1 h 36 min
43 20:32

44–46

Ordinary price	Sale price
£20.00	**£16.00**
£35.00	**£28.00**
£60.00	**£48.00**

47 FALSE
48 TRUE
49 TRUE
50 TRUE

Paper 11

1 Line B
2 20
3 50
4 10:30 a.m.
5 9 a.m.
6 11:30 a.m.
7 50 km
8 £65
9 15
10 $\frac{5}{6}$
11 $\frac{3}{4}$
12 $\frac{2}{3}$
13 $\frac{1}{2}$
14 $\frac{3}{8}$
15 40
16 50
17 35
18 16
19 13
20 none
21 A
22 B
23 none
24 C

25 $\frac{3}{8}$
26 0.23
27 0.09
28 5
29–33

34–35 $(-3, 3)$
36–37 $(-1, 1)$
38 2620
39 890
40 2516
41 84
42 42
43 21
44 60
45 30
46 15
47 0.0342
48 0.0086
49 0.2746
50 0.003

Paper 12

1 337
2 427
3 517
4 607
5 697
6 10^4
7 7^3
8 5^5
9 1^6
10 4^4
11 11^5
12 1
13 63 m^2
14 32 m
15 D
16 A
17 F
18 0.822
19 0.806
20 0.798
21 6
22 1
23 Tuesday
24 Thursday
25 98.4 °F
26 English
27 Geography
28 Art
29 Mathematics
30 History
31 French
32 22
33 27

34 0.5
35 0.05
36 $15\frac{1}{2}$
37 $23\frac{1}{2}$
38 1
39 1.1
40 0.625
41 0.75
42–43 16, 17
44 17
45 2
46 16.8
47 16
48 16
49 2
50 16.6

Paper 13

1–3

4 $\frac{2}{5}$
5 0.07
6 7
7 7
8 4
9 25 cm
10 0.001
11 $\frac{1}{2}$
12 £2
13 £1
14 £0.40
15 80p
16 9.99
17 6.837
18 1.511
19 47
20 2750
21 38 200
22 125
23 875
24 30
25 1
26 3
27 1
28 3
29 3
30 2

31–40

×	(5)	(4)	(9)	(2)
(2)	**10**	8	18	**4**
(3)	**15**	12	**27**	**6**
(7)	35	**28**	**63**	14
(1)	**5**	**4**	**9**	2

41 20
42 77
43 56
44 12
45 36
46 49
47 0.84
48 27
49 9
50 3

Paper 14

1–3

60	144	72	**132**	120
5	12	**6**	11	**10**

4 4.18
5 0.57
6 278
7 10
8 5
9 5 km
10 12 km/h
11 72
12 12
13 3
14 2
15 16
16 12
17 6
18 128
19 131
20 132
21 129
22   132
  9)1188
23 4:04 p.m.
24 216
25 288
26 234
27 282
28 264
29 60°
30 120°
31 30°
32 45°

33–43

	Begins	Ends
1st lesson	**09:15**	**09:35**
2nd lesson	**09:55**	**10:35**
Break	**10:35**	**10:50**
3rd lesson	**10:50**	**11:30**
4th lesson	**11:30**	**12:10**
5th lesson	**12:10**	12:50

44 350
45 280
46 16
47 4
48 5 kg
49 250 g or 2.5 kg
50 £4.20

Paper 15

1 26
2 26
3 27
4 28
5 26
6 17
7 £6
8 15
9 13
10 6
11 2
12 16
13 Long Mitton
14 Boston
15 (1, 4)
16 (3, 5)
17 20 km
18 40 km
19 FORWARD 4
20 LEFT 90°
21 FORWARD 3
22 RIGHT 90°
23 FORWARD 2
24 Phone with camera, no MP3 player
25 Phone with MP3 player, no camera
26 Does it have an MP3 player?
27 Does it have a camera?
28 FALSE
29 TRUE
30 FALSE
31 23
32 191
33 173
34 10 989

35–38

	Length	Width	Area	Perimeter
Rectangle 1	7 m	4 m	**28 m²**	**22 m**
Rectangle 2	9 m	**4 m**	36 m²	**26 m**

39 47
40 65
41 6.7
42 7.2
43 5

44 $6\frac{1}{2}$
45 1
46 10
47 59
48 52
49 $\frac{5}{8}$
50 $\frac{3}{4}$

Paper 16

1 75%
2 $\frac{1}{4}$
3 8
4 24
5 9
6 144
7 48
8 2
9 1000 m²
10 2800 m²
11 1800 m²
12 140 m
13 220 m
14 £2.49
15 B
16 A
17 NONE
18 C
19 1
20 14
21 0.0342
22 0.0086
23 0.2746
24 0.003
25 72
26 36
27 18
28 75
29 31
30 20
31 48
32 24
33 36
34 18
35 18
36 23
37 235
38 218
39 $\frac{1}{2}$
40 $\frac{9}{10}$
41 92
42 5
43 2
44 20
45 12
46 $\frac{1}{16}$
47 13
48 17
49 2
50 3

Paper 17

1 80%
2 60%
3 85%
4 90%
5 70%
6 33
7 66%
8 9
9 28
10 44
11 49
12 13
13 93
14 62%
15 8
16 1
17 4
18 0
19 32
20 16
21 8
22 cube
23 triangular-based pyramid
24 cuboid
25 triangular prism
26 30 275
27 thirty thousand two hundred and seventy-five

28–37

	Length	Width	Perimeter	Area
Rectangle 1	29 m	**1 m**	60 m	**29 m²**
Rectangle 2	28 m	**2 m**	60 m	**56 m²**
Rectangle 3	**25 m**	5 m	60 m	**125 m²**
Rectangle 4	**20 m**	10 m	60 m	**200 m²**
Rectangle 5	15 m	**15 m**	60 m	**225 m²**

38 2.27
39 125 g
40 300 g
41 11 eggs
42 km
43 litres
44 tonnes
45 mm
46 0.7
47 0.707
48 0.708
49 0.77
50 0.78

Paper 18

1 22
2 53
3 £4.20

4–15

£	US Dollars	Kenyan Shillings	Euros	Australian Dollars
£10.00	**14.60**	**1190**	**14.2**	**21.30**
£5.00	**7.30**	**595**	**7.1**	**10.65**
£0.50	**0.73**	**59.50**	**0.71**	**1.065**

16 7.88
17 7.8
18 7.088
19 7.008

20–25

Fraction	Decimal	Percentage
$\frac{1}{2}$	**0.5**	**50%**
$\frac{1}{4}$	0.25	**25%**
$\frac{1}{5}$	0.2	**20%**

26 7
27 7
28 8
29 12
30 63
31 3
32 9
33 34.6
34 $\frac{1}{4}$
35 1 h 4 min or 64 min
36 A
37 38 min
38 18:09
39 10:00 p.m.
40 2:30 p.m.
41 1:30 p.m.
42 12:15 p.m.
43 5:30 p.m.
44 41 years 8 months
45–46 10 years 5 months
47 56 cm
48 36 cm
49 60 cm
50 127 cm

Paper 19

1 $7\frac{4}{5}$
2 $47\frac{1}{2}$
3 $31\frac{1}{4}$
4 $\frac{1}{8}$
5 2650 m

6–13

×	(5)	(7)	(2)	(3)
(3)	**15**	**21**	6	9
(8)	**40**	56	16	24
(4)	20	**28**	8	12
(9)	45	63	**18**	27

14 1.7
15 1.43
16 47
17 0.007
18 2590
19 0.14
20 ×
21 ×
22 +
23 −
24 −
25 ÷
26 100
27 1.23
28 13.6
29 4.4

30–35

Price before VAT	VAT	Total price
£500	**£87.50**	**£587.50**
£150	**£26.25**	**£176.25**
£60	**£10.50**	**£70.50**

36–41

	Length	Width	Perimeter	Area
Piece A	8 cm	**3** cm	**22** cm	24 cm²
Piece B	**6** cm	4 cm	**20** cm	24 cm²
Piece C	12 cm	**2** cm	**28** cm	24 cm²

42 50%
43 16%
44 no
45 yes
46 no
47 no
48 no
49 no
50 yes

Paper 20

1–2 Laser, Spaceship
3–4 Galaxy, Spaceship
5 £8.60
6 £2.15

7 29%
8 5121
9 4021
10 8080
11 433

12–14

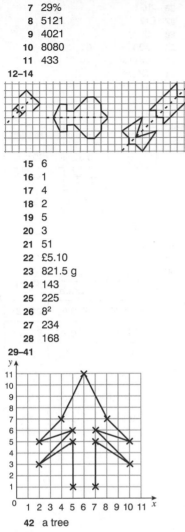

15 6
16 1
17 4
18 2
19 5
20 3
21 51
22 £5.10
23 821.5 g
24 143
25 225
26 8^2
27 234
28 168

29–41

42 a tree

43–48

Ocean	Square km	Square miles
Atlantic	82 200 000	31 700 000
Indian	73 480 000	28 360 000
Pacific	165 000 000	64 000 000

49 70
50 490

Paper 21

1 even
2 odd
3 even
4 even
5 £2
6 £3
7 £5
8 £6

9 £8
10 45p
11 1 h 10 min
12 1 h 35 min
13 2 h 0 min
14 2 h 25 min
15 2 h 50 min
16 3 h 15 min
17 0.374
18 0.0148
19 0.00255
20 189
21 231
22 £4.80
23 £3
24 £1.20
25 $\frac{5}{6}$
26 $\frac{3}{4}$
27 $\frac{7}{12}$
28 $\frac{11}{24}$
29 $\frac{3}{8}$
30 mile
31 pint or fluid ounce
32 ounce
33 feet
34 8:20 p.m.
35 8:05 a.m.
36 12:10 a.m.
37 5:45 p.m.
38 53
39 9
40 10
41 9
42 £1.05
43 14
44 42
45 84
46 12
47 33
48 3
49 9
50 6

Paper 22

1 22 m
2 5.5 m
3 Ben
4 Ahmed
5 7
6 Ben
7 3
8 Ahmed
9 14
10 13
11 14
12 12
13 0.7

14 7
15 70
16 4230
17 4230
18 5230
19 77
20 75
21 53
22 49
23 45
24 51
25 64
26 49

27–32

33 10:23
34 10:37
35 10:50
36 11:04
37 11:29
38 LEFT 90°
39 FORWARD 1
40 FORWARD 1
41 LEFT 90°
42 RIGHT 90°
43 FORWARD 2
44 125.75 m
45 56 days
46 £495
47 64
48 120
49 73
50 6

Paper 23

1–10

×	(11)	(9)	(6)	(4)
(8)	**88**	**72**	48	**32**
(5)	**55**	**45**	30	**20**
(1)	11	9	**6**	**4**
(6)	66	**54**	**36**	24

11 71 200
12 1500
13 1300
14 700

15	121
16	12
17	177
18	205
19	143 400

20–23

a	0	1	2	3
♣	3	4	5	6

24	17
25	40
26	12
27	9
28	15 cm^2
29	14 cm^2
30	20 cm^2
31	15 cm^2
32	73
33	292
34	14th March
35	48 kg
36	6 kg

37–40

a	2	35	77	47	89
3a	6	105	231	141	267

41	311
42	162
43	18
44	£4.70
45	£16.45
46	171

47	3.125
48	4.05
49	7.625
50	9.075

Paper 24

1	$\frac{7}{12}$
2	8.01
3	0.016
4	200
5	1.789
6	540
7	49 cm^2
8	7203

9–15

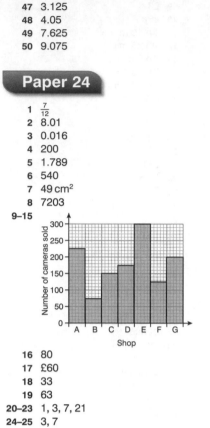

16	80
17	£60
18	33
19	63
20–23	1, 3, 7, 21
24–25	3, 7

26	29
27	£17
28	10
29	1000 or 10 000
30	256 cm^2
31	112 cm^2
32	144 cm^2
33	64 cm
34	64 cm

35–42

Fraction	Decimal	Percentage
$\frac{3}{10}$	0.3	30%
$\frac{7}{100}$	0.07	7%
$\frac{1}{4}$	0.25	25%
$\frac{1}{20}$	0.05	5%

43	6.873
44	19.05

45–50

Wholesale price	Retail price	Profit
£18.75	£23.50	£11.31
£4.75	£70.20	£11.35
£5.13	£6.10	97p
£196.50	£235.25	£1.12
£58.85	£13.50	£2.19
93p	£38.75	19p

44–46 The ages of Grandad, Uncle John and Tom add up to 105 years.

B 13

Grandad is twice as old as Uncle John, and Uncle John is twice as old as Tom.

Grandad is _____ years old, Uncle John is _____ years old and Tom is _____ years old.

3

Divide each of the following by 1000.

B 1

47 34.2 _____

48 8.6 _____

49 274.6 _____

50 3 _____

4

Now go to the Progress Chart to record your score! Total ◯ 50

Paper 12

1–5 Write down the numbers that will come out of this machine

B 9

| 34 | 43 | 52 | 61 | 70 | ×10 | −3 |

5

$5 \times 5 = 5^2$ $2 \times 2 \times 2 = 2^3$. Now write the following in the same way.

B 6

6 $10 \times 10 \times 10 \times 10 =$ _____

7 $7 \times 7 \times 7 =$ _____

8 $5 \times 5 \times 5 \times 5 \times 5 =$ _____

9 $1 \times 1 \times 1 \times 1 \times 1 \times 1 =$ _____

10 $4 \times 4 \times 4 \times 4 =$ _____

11 $11 \times 11 \times 11 \times 11 \times 11 =$ _____

12 What number is $1 \times 1 \times 1 \times 1 \times 1 \times 1$? _____

7

B 20

13 Find the area of a hall which is 9 metres long and 7 metres wide. _____

14 What is the perimeter of the hall? _____

2

At the supermarket there were various sizes of *Marvello*.

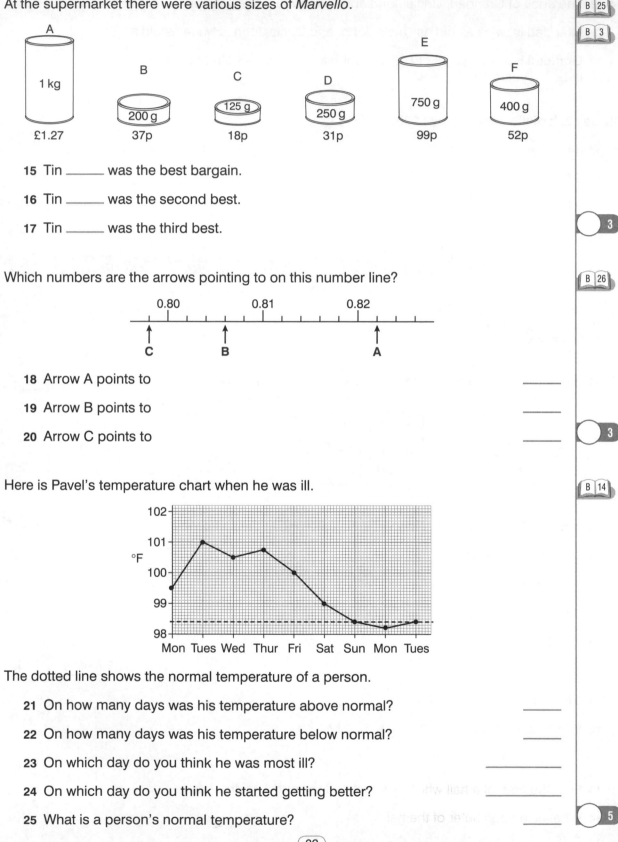

B 25

B 3

15 Tin _____ was the best bargain.

16 Tin _____ was the second best.

17 Tin _____ was the third best.

3

Which numbers are the arrows pointing to on this number line?

B 26

18 Arrow A points to   _____

19 Arrow B points to   _____

20 Arrow C points to   _____

3

Here is Pavel's temperature chart when he was ill.

B 14

The dotted line shows the normal temperature of a person.

21 On how many days was his temperature above normal?   _____

22 On how many days was his temperature below normal?   _____

23 On which day do you think he was most ill?   _____

24 On which day do you think he started getting better?   _____

25 What is a person's normal temperature?   _____

5

In the end-of-term tests Zanna got the following marks.

Mathematics	$\frac{54}{75}$	English	$\frac{48}{60}$
History	$\frac{27}{40}$	French	$\frac{25}{40}$
Geography	$\frac{39}{50}$	Art	$\frac{15}{20}$

26 Her best subject was _____

27 2nd was _____

28 3rd was _____

29 4th was _____

30 5th was _____

31 6th was _____

B 10

6

Complete these sequences.

B 7

32–33 12   13   15   18   _____   _____

34–35 5000   500   50   5   _____   _____

36–37 8 $8\frac{1}{2}$ $9\frac{1}{2}$ $11\frac{1}{2}$ _____   _____

38–39 0.6   0.7   0.8   0.9   _____   _____

40–41 0.125   0.25   0.375   0.5   _____   _____

B11/B10

10

Here are the scores in a mental arithmetic test out of 20.

B 15

Name	Peter	Cressida	Petra	Greg	Helen
Score	17	16	18	16	17

42–43 There are two modes: what are they? _____ _____

44 What is the **median**? _____

45 What is the **range**? _____

46 What is the **mean**? _____

Peter's test was wrongly marked and he should have got 16 not 17.

47 Which score is the **mode** now? _____

48 What is the **median** now? _____

49 What is the **range** now? _____

50 What is the **mean** now? _____

9

Paper 13

1–3 Complete the figures below. The dotted line is the line of symmetry.

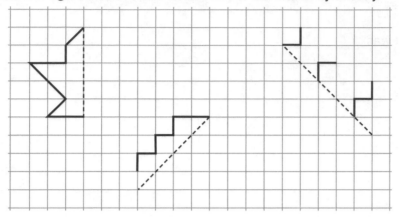

B 24

3

Underline the correct answer in each line.

4 $\frac{1}{5} + \frac{2}{10}$ = $\frac{3}{15}$ $\frac{2}{5}$ $\frac{3}{10}$ $\frac{5}{10}$ $\frac{1}{5}$

5 $0.49 \div 7$ = 7   0.7   0.07   70   700

6 20% of 35 = 7   8   15   20   25

7 $4^2 - 3^2$ = 1   2   3   7   9

8 $2^3 - 2^2$ = 1   2   3   4   5

9 25% of 1 metre = 1 cm   2 cm   10 cm   25 cm   25 m

10 $0.1 \times 0.1 \times 0.1$ = 0.3   0.2   0.001   0.003   0.0001

11 $\frac{1}{3} + \frac{1}{6}$ = $\frac{2}{3}$ $\frac{1}{2}$ $\frac{1}{9}$ $\frac{2}{9}$ $\frac{1}{18}$

B 10
B 11
B 12
B 6
B 6
B12/B25
B 11
B 10

8

12–14 Share £3.40 among Angela, Maya and Claire. For every 10p Angela gets, Maya gets 5p, and Claire gets 2p.

Angela gets _____, Maya gets _____ and Claire gets _____ .

B 13

3

15 $\frac{3}{4}$ of a sum of money is £1.80. What is $\frac{1}{3}$ of it? _____

16 Multiply 3.7 by itself, and then take 3.7 from the answer. _____

17 Add together 3.7, 2.95 and 0.187. _____

18 Take 1.689 from 3.2. _____

19 Divide 799 by 17. _____

B10/B3
B 11
B11/B2
B11/B2
B 3

5

Multiply each of the numbers below by 1000.

B 1

20 2.75 _____

21 38.2 _____

22 0.125 _____

23 0.875 _____

4

The bar chart below shows the marks in Mathematics for Class 8.

B 14
B 10

The maximum mark was 100.
One boy gained over 90.

$\frac{2}{5}$ of those who received between 81 and 90 were girls.

$\frac{3}{4}$ of those who received between 71 and 80 were boys.

$\frac{1}{2}$ of those who received between 61 and 70 were girls.

$\frac{1}{3}$ of those who received between 51 and 60 were girls.

$\frac{1}{2}$ of those who received between 41 and 50 were boys.

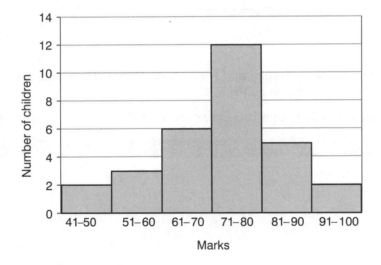

24 How many children took the test? _____

25 How many girls got over 90 marks? _____

26 How many boys received between 61 and 70 marks? _____

27 How many girls received between 41 and 50 marks? _____

28 In the 81 to 90 mark range, how many were boys? _____

29 In the 71 to 80 mark range, how many were girls? _____

30 How many boys received between 51 and 60 marks? _____

7

31–40 Fill in the multiplication table.

×				
	___	8	18	___
	___	12	___	___
	35	___	___	14
	___	___	___	2

Fill in the missing numbers.

41 $\dfrac{4}{5} = \dfrac{\quad}{25}$

42 $\dfrac{7}{11} = \dfrac{\quad}{121}$

43 $\dfrac{7}{8} = \dfrac{\quad}{64}$

44 $\dfrac{2}{7} = \dfrac{\quad}{42}$

45 $\dfrac{3}{4} = \dfrac{\quad}{48}$

46 $\dfrac{7}{9} = \dfrac{\quad}{63}$

47 If 13 items cost £1.56, what would 7 items cost?　　　　£ _____

48–50 Share 39 sweets among Penny, Ragini and Prue giving Penny 3 times as much as Ragini, and Ragini 3 times as much as Prue.

Penny has _____ sweets, Ragini has _____ sweets, and Prue has _____ sweets.

Now go to the Progress Chart to record your score!　　Total　　50

Paper 14

1–3 Complete this table.

60	144	72		120
5	12	___	11	___

4　　$\begin{array}{r} 0.38 \\ \times\ 11 \\ \hline \\ \hline \end{array}$

5　　$9\overline{)5.13}$

6　　$\begin{array}{r} 1030 \\ -\ 752 \\ \hline \\ \hline \end{array}$

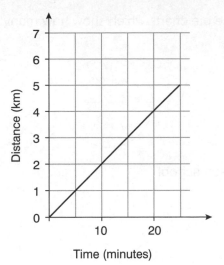

Time (minutes)

Look at the line graph and then answer these questions.

7 I'll do 2 km in _____ minutes.

8 I'll do 1 km in _____ minutes.

9 How far will I travel in 25 minutes? _____

10 What is my speed in km/h? _____

11 What number, when multiplied by 25, gives the same answer as 45×40? _____

Solve these equations.

12 $3 + a = 15$
$a =$ _____

13 $x + 4 = 7$
$x =$ _____

14 $5 + a = 7$
$a =$ _____

15 $y - 7 = 9$
$y =$ _____

16 $b - 4 = 8$
$b =$ _____

17 $c - 1 = 5$
$c =$ _____

18–21 Do these divisions.

$7\overline{)896}$ $6\overline{)786}$ $9\overline{)1188}$ $4\overline{)516}$

22 Circle the division with the largest **quotient**.

It takes me 19 minutes to walk home from school.

23 If I leave school at 3:45 p.m. what time will I get home? _____

24 How many minutes are there from 10:29 p.m. on Monday to 2:05 a.m. on Tuesday? _____ minutes

B 14
B 3
4
B 3
1
B 8
6
B 3
5
B 27
2

Four schools in Sandville made these pie charts which show how many of their pupils walk to school.

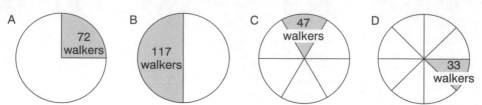

Write the total number of pupils in each school.

25 School A _____

26 School B _____

27 School C _____

28 School D _____

29 Angle x = _____

30 Angle $2x$ = _____

31 Angle a = _____

32 Angle b = _____

Complete the timetable below.

33–43 There are five 40-minute lessons, with a break of 15 minutes after the second lesson.

	Begins	**Ends**
1st lesson	_____	_____
2nd lesson	_____	_____
Break	_____	_____
3rd lesson	_____	_____
4th lesson	_____	_____
5th lesson	_____	12:50

44–45 There are 630 children in a school. There are 5 boys to every 4 girls.

There are _____ boys and _____ girls.

B 14 B 2 B 3 4 B 17 4 B 27 11 B 13 2

46–47 The perimeter of a rectangle is 40 cm. The length is 4 times the width.

The length is _____ cm and the width is _____ cm.

B 20
2

1 kg of *Britewash* costs £1.20. At this price per kg:

B 3

48 I could buy _____ with £6.00.

B 25

49 I could buy _____ with 30p.

50 I would have to pay _____ for 3.5 kg.

3

Now go to the Progress Chart to record your score! **Total** 50

Paper 15

Here are the scores in a Science test out of 50.

B 15

Name	Kamala	Matt	Rashid	Jo	James
Score	42	15	26	31	26

1 What is the **mode**? _____

2 What is the **median**? _____

3 What is the **range**? _____

4 What is the **mean**? _____

Matt actually got 25 not 15.

5 What is the median now? _____

6 What is the range now? _____

6

After I had bought a book costing £2.40, one third of what I had left was £1.20.

B4/B3

7 How much money did I have at first? _____

B 2

1

There are 24 children in our class. This Venn diagram shows how many of us belong to the Cycling Club (C) and how many of us belong to the Swimming Club (S).

B 14
B 2

8 How many belong to the Cycling Club? _____

9 How many belong to the Swimming Club? _____

10 How many belong to both clubs ? _____

11 How many belong to neither club? _____

12 How many belong to one club only? _____

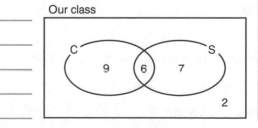

Our class

C 9 6 7 S

2

5

(39)

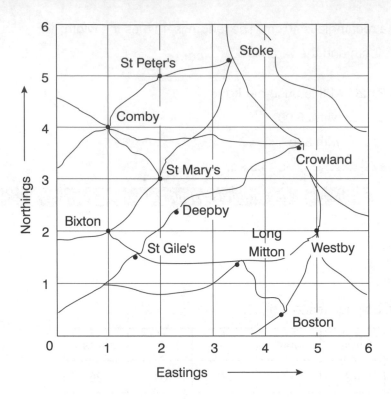

This map is covered with a grid, the lines of which are numbered 0−6 for eastings and 0−6 for northings. The position of towns is found by giving their **coordinates**, e.g. Bixton is (1, 2).

Some of the towns are not situated on the lines, but are inside the squares.

When this is so, the **coordinates** of the bottom left-hand corner of the square are given, e.g. Deepby is (2, 2).

Scale: A side of a small square represents 10 km.

Name the towns which are at the following positions.

13 (3, 1) _____

14 (4, 0) _____

Give the **coordinates** for the following towns.

15 Comby (_____ , _____)

16 Stoke (_____ , _____)

Approximately, how far is it, as the crow flies (in a straight line), from:

17 St Gile's to Long Mitton? _____

18 Bixton to Westby? _____

6

40

Your task is to guide the robot along the white squares on the plan.
It starts and finishes on one of the squares marked A, B, C, D or E.
It can only move FORWARD, turn RIGHT 90° and turn LEFT 90°.

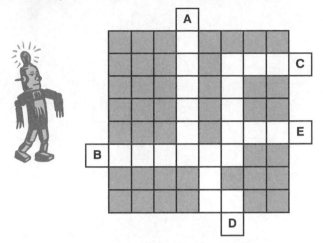

Complete these instructions to guide the robot along the white squares.

19 From A to B: FORWARD 6, RIGHT 90°, _____ .

20 From B to C: FORWARD 6, _____, FORWARD 4, RIGHT 90°, FORWARD 3.

21 From C to E: FORWARD 3, LEFT 90°, _____, LEFT 90°, FORWARD 3.

22–23 From D to B: FORWARD 1, LEFT 90°, FORWARD 1, _____, _____,
LEFT 90°, FORWARD 5.

5

24–27 Jada used this decision tree to sort mobile phones. What is missing from the tree?
Fill in the gaps.

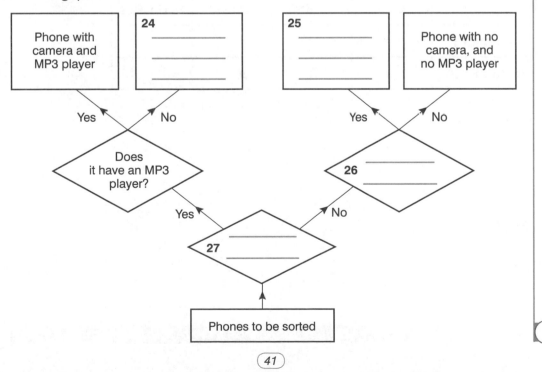

4

41

State whether the following statements are TRUE or FALSE.

28 Line B is parallel to line C. _____

29 Line B is perpendicular to line C. _____

30 Line B is a horizontal line. _____

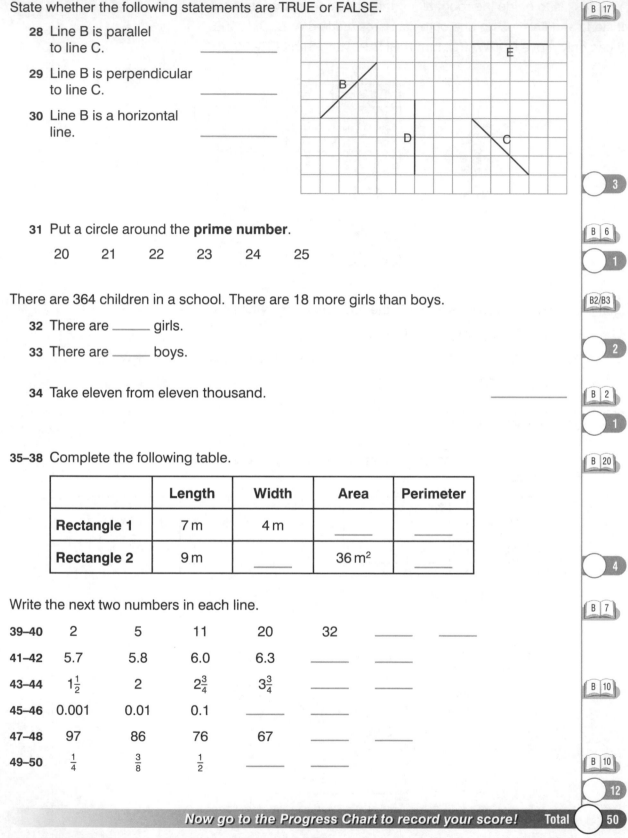

3

31 Put a circle around the **prime number**.

20 21 22 23 24 25

B 6

1

There are 364 children in a school. There are 18 more girls than boys.

B2/B3

32 There are _____ girls.

33 There are _____ boys.

2

34 Take eleven from eleven thousand. _____

B 2

1

35–38 Complete the following table.

B 20

	Length	Width	Area	Perimeter
Rectangle 1	7 m	4 m	_____	_____
Rectangle 2	9 m	_____	36 m²	_____

4

Write the next two numbers in each line.

B 7

39–40	2	5	11	20	32	_____	_____
41–42	5.7	5.8	6.0	6.3	_____	_____
43–44	$1\frac{1}{2}$	2	$2\frac{3}{4}$	$3\frac{3}{4}$	_____	_____
45–46	0.001	0.01	0.1	_____	_____
47–48	97	86	76	67	_____	_____
49–50	$\frac{1}{4}$	$\frac{3}{8}$	$\frac{1}{2}$	_____	_____

B 10

B 10

12

Now go to the Progress Chart to record your score!   Total   50

Paper 16

Here is a pie chart which shows how many computers pupils in Class 6C have at home.

- No computer
- One computer
- More than one computer

1 What percentage of pupils have at least one computer at home? _____

2 What fraction of pupils have more than one computer at home? _____

If there are 32 pupils in Class 6C:

3 How many do not have a computer at home? _____

4 How many have at least one computer at home? _____

5 Find the smallest number which must be added to 890 to make it exactly divisible by 31. _____

6 Find the sum of 47, 48 and 49. _____

7 Find the **mean** of 47, 48 and 49. _____

8 Find the **range** of 47, 48 and 49. _____

Our school swimming pool, which is 50 m long and 20 m wide, has a path 10 m wide all around it.

Wall

Wall   20 m   50 m   Wall

Wall

9 What is the area of the swimming pool? _____

10 What is the area of the whole complex (swimming pool and the path)? _____

11 What is the area of the path? _____

12 What is the perimeter of the swimming pool? _____

13 What is the total length of the wall? _____

14 Jenny bought 7 metres of material. She gave the assistant £20.00 and received £2.57 change.

What was the price of the material per metre? _____

43

Here are three shaded cubes.

A   B   C

Which cube has the following nets? Choose between A, B, C or none.

15   Is _____

16   Is _____

17   Is _____

18   Is _____

What number is represented by the symbol in each equation?

19 $10 - ✹ = 27 ÷ 3$
$✹ =$ _____

20 $3 + ✈ = 20 - 3$
$✈ =$ _____

Divide each number by 1000.

21 34.2 _____

22 8.6 _____

23 274.6 _____

24 3 _____

Tim, Carl and Lewis had 126 cards. Carl won 3 from Tim, and Lewis lost 2 to Carl. They then found that Tim had twice as many as Carl, and Carl had twice as many as Lewis.

25–27 At the end of the game Tim had _____ , Carl had _____ and Lewis had _____ .

28–30 At the start of the game Tim had _____ , Carl had _____ and Lewis had _____ .

We asked 144 children at our school how they spent their holiday.

When we got their answers we made this pie chart.

31 How many children went to the beach? _____

32 How many went sailing? _____

33 The number of children who went on an Activity holiday was _____

34 How many went camping? _____

35 How many went canal boating? _____

Beach

Sailing

60°

45° Canal boat

Activity holiday

Camping

4

B8/B3
B 2
2

B 1
4

B4/B13
B 2
6

B 14
B 3
5

In a school there were a total of 476 pupils and teachers.

The girls + the teachers = 241   The boys + the teachers = 258

36–38 There were _____ teachers, _____ boys and _____ girls.

B 2
3

Underline the correct answer in each line.

39 $\frac{1}{3} + \frac{1}{6}$ $=$ $\frac{2}{3}$ $\frac{1}{2}$ $\frac{1}{9}$ $\frac{2}{9}$ $\frac{1}{6}$

40 $\frac{1}{5} + \frac{7}{10}$ $=$ $\frac{8}{10}$ $\frac{8}{15}$ $\frac{9}{15}$ $\frac{11}{15}$ $\frac{9}{10}$

41 $111 - 19$ $=$ 100 128 102 82 92

42 $6 \div 1.2$ $=$ 48 5 50 0.5 5.3

43 $3^3 - 5^2$ $=$ 8 15 3 2 1

44 $60 \div 3$ $=$ 4 8 20 32 57

45 25% of 48 $=$ 12 24 25 48 60

46 $\frac{1}{4} \times \frac{1}{4}$ $=$ 1 $\frac{1}{8}$ $\frac{1}{16}$ $\frac{1}{2}$ $\frac{1}{6}$

B 10
B 10
B 2
B 3
B 6
B 3
B 12
B 10
8

47–48 Put a circle around the **prime numbers**.

13   14   15   16   17

49–50 Underline the **prime factors** of 18.

2   3   4   5   6   7   8

B 6
B 5
4

Now go to the Progress Chart to record your score!   Total   50

Paper 17

1–5 Here are Ajay's exam marks. Change them into percentages.

Subject	Actual mark	Possible mark	Percentage
Science	12	15	_____
French	21	35	_____
English	68	80	_____
Art	63	70	_____
Music	14	20	_____

B 12
B 2
B 15

6 Ajay's total mark in Science and French was _____ out of 50.

7 What is Ajay's total mark in Science and French expressed as a percentage? _____

7

8–12 Write down Peter's actual marks.

Subject	Actual mark	Possible mark	Percentage
Science	_____	15	60
French	_____	35	80
English	_____	80	55
Art	_____	70	70
Music	_____	20	65

13 Peter's total mark in English and Art was _____ out of 150.

14 What is Peter's total mark in English and Art expressed as a percentage? _____

Write each of these numbers to the nearest whole number.

15 8.35 _____   **16** 0.71 _____

17 4.48 _____   **18** 0.123 _____

19–21 There are 56 beads. Sam has twice as many as Ren, who has twice as many as Aisha.

Sam has _____ beads, Ren has _____ beads and Aisha has _____ beads.

These are the nets of solids. What solids will they make? Choose four from: square-based pyramid, triangular-based pyramid, triangular prism, pentagonal prism, cube, cuboid, sphere or cone.

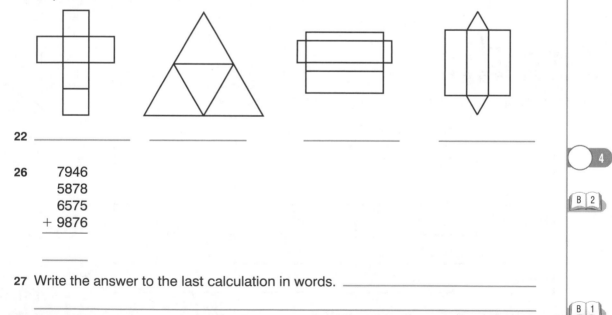

22 _____ _____ _____ _____

26
```
   7946
   5878
   6575
 + 9876
 _____

 _____
```

27 Write the answer to the last calculation in words. _____

_____

46

28–37 Complete the following chart.

	Length	Width	Perimeter	Area
Rectangle 1	29 m	___	60 m	___
Rectangle 2	28 m	___	60 m	___
Rectangle 3	___	5 m	60 m	___
Rectangle 4	___	10 m	60 m	___
Rectangle 5	15 m	___	60 m	___

38 Multiply 0.0908 by 25. _____

39–41 Convert this recipe for pasta from imperial to metric units (to the nearest 5 g).

Use the approximation: 1 oz = 25 g

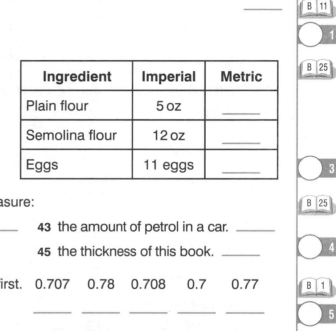

Ingredient	Imperial	Metric
Plain flour	5 oz	___
Semolina flour	12 oz	___
Eggs	11 eggs	___

Give the most appropriate metric unit to measure:

42 the distance from Earth to the Sun. _____   **43** the amount of petrol in a car. _____

44 the weight of a train. _____   **45** the thickness of this book. _____

46–50 Put these numbers in order, smallest first.   0.707   0.78   0.708   0.7   0.77

_____ _____ _____ _____ _____

Now go to the Progress Chart to record your score!   **Total**   50

Paper 18

1 In a class, 19 children have dogs and 18 children have cats.

If 15 children have both dogs and cats, find the smallest possible number of children in the class. _____

2 How many times can 27 be subtracted from 1431? _____

3 Twelve toys were bought for £1.25 each and sold for £1.60 each.

What was the total profit? _____

4–15 Here are some exchange rates.

£1 = 1.46 US Dollars
£1 = 119 Kenyan Shillings
£1 = 1.42 Euros
£1 = 2.13 Australian Dollars

Complete the table.

£	US Dollars	Kenyan Shillings	Euros	Australian Dollars
£10.00	____	____	____	____
£5.00	____	____	____	____
£0.50	____	____	____	____

16–19 Arrange these numbers in order, putting the largest first.

7.8   7.088   7.88   7.008   ____   ____   ____   ____

20–25 Complete the following table.

Fraction	Decimal	Percentage
$\frac{1}{2}$	____	____
____	0.25	____
$\frac{1}{5}$	____	____

26–30 Solve these equations.

$\dfrac{56}{a} = 8$ $\dfrac{49}{b} = 7$ $\dfrac{72}{9} = x$ $\dfrac{y}{4} = 3$ $\dfrac{z}{9} = 7$

$a = $ ____ $b = $ ____ $x = $ ____ $y = $ ____ $z = $ ____

31 The product of two numbers is 111.

The larger number is 37. What is the other number?   ____

What are the missing numbers in these number squares?

49	36	25
36	25	16
25	16	x

y	30.2	25.8
30.2	25.8	21.4
25.8	21.4	17

$\frac{1}{2}$	$\frac{5}{8}$	$\frac{3}{4}$
$\frac{3}{8}$	$\frac{1}{2}$	$\frac{5}{8}$
z	$\frac{3}{8}$	$\frac{1}{2}$

32 $x = $ ____   **33** $y = $ ____   **34** $z = $ ____

48

B 3
B 13

12

B 1

4

B 10
B 11
B 12

6

B 8
B 10

5

B 3

1

B 7

3

	Train A	Train B	Train C	Train D
Westbury	08:11	09:20	18:09	20:09
Trowbridge	08:19	09:30	17:58	20:04
Bath	08:45	09:54	17:23	19:31
Bristol	09:00	10:11	17:05	19:17

35 How long does the slowest train take to do the entire journey? _____

36 If I live in Westbury, and want to be in Bath before 9 a.m., on which train must I travel? _____

37 How long does the 19:31 from Bath take to travel to Westbury? _____

38 When should the 17:23 from Bath arrive in Westbury? _____

Using this world time chart answer the following questions.

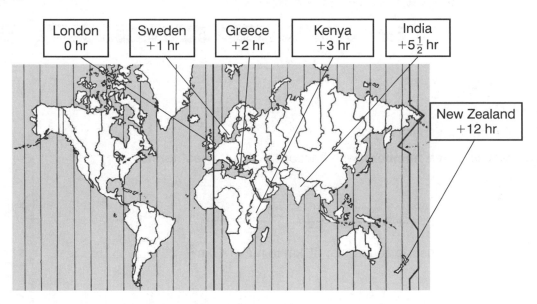

London 0 hr
Sweden +1 hr
Greece +2 hr
Kenya +3 hr
India +5½ hr
New Zealand +12 hr

39 When it is 10:00 a.m. in London, what time is it in New Zealand? _____

40 When it is 9:00 a.m. in London, what time is it in India? _____

41 When it is 3:30 p.m. in Greece, what time is it in London? _____

42 When it is 1:15 p.m. in Sweden, what time is it in London? _____

43 If I made a telephone call from Kenya to India at 3:00 p.m., what time would it be in India? _____

	Years	Months
Tony is	10	8
Claire is	9	6
Abdel is	11	4
Mandy is	10	2

B 2
B 15

44 Look at the table. The children's ages add up to _____ years _____ months

45–46 What is the **mean** age of the four children? _____ years _____ months

3

Here is a box 20 cm long, 10 cm wide, and 8 cm high.

A ribbon is placed round the box, once lengthwise, and once round the width.

B 20
B 2

47 What is the perimeter of the side of the box? _____

48 What is the perimeter of the end of the box? _____

49 What is the perimeter of the base of the box? _____

50 If I allow 35 cm for the bow, how much ribbon will I need? _____

4

Now go to the Progress Chart to record your score! **Total** 50

Paper 19

Divide each of the numbers below by 10.

Give your answers as **mixed numbers**, with fractions in their **lowest terms**.

B 3
B 10

1 78 _____   **2** 475 _____

3 312.5 _____   **4** 1.25 _____

4

5 How many metres must be added to 1.35 km to make 4 km? _____

B 25

1

6–13 Fill in the multiplication grid.

B 3

×				
	__	__	6	9
	__	56	16	24
	20	__	__	__
	45	63	__	__

8

Write each of these values in decimal form.

14 17 tenths _____

15 143 hundredths _____

16 47 units _____

17 7 thousandths _____

18 259 tens _____

19 14 hundredths _____

B 11

6

Insert signs to make the following correct.

20–22 5 _____ 5 _____ 1 = 13 _____ 12

23–25 (7 _____ 4) _____ 2 = 25 _____ 25

B3/B2

6

Insert the missing numbers in these calculations.

26 $4.9 \times$ _____ $= 490$

27 _____ $\div 10 = 0.123$

28 $0.136 \times 100 =$ _____

B1/B3

3

29 The average of 6 numbers is 4.

If one of the numbers is 2, what is the average of the other 5 numbers? _____

B 15

1

30–35 VAT (Value Added Tax) is added to the price of some goods.

It is charged at $17\frac{1}{2}\%$ (£17.50 on each £100).

Complete the following table.

Price before VAT	VAT	Total price
£500	_____	_____
£150	_____	_____
£60	_____	_____

B12/B2

6

36–41 Three rectangular pieces of card have the same area (24 cm²).

Fill in the other measurements.

	Length	Width	Perimeter	Area
Piece A	8 cm	_____ cm	_____ cm	24 cm²
Piece B	_____ cm	4 cm	_____ cm	24 cm²
Piece C	12 cm	_____ cm	_____ cm	24 cm²

B 20

6

What percentages are the following fractions?

42 $\frac{15}{30} =$ _____

43 $\frac{4}{25} =$ _____

B12/B10

2

Look at the diagram. Answer the questions below by writing YES or NO.

It would help you if you drew in the diagonals with a ruler.

B 17
B 19

44 Are all the sides the same length? _____

45 Are the opposite sides parallel? _____

46 Are all the angles equal? _____

47 Are the diagonals the same length? _____

48 Do the diagonals cross at right angles? _____

49 Is this a **rhombus**? _____

50 Is this a **parallelogram**? _____   **7**

Now go to the Progress Chart to record your score!   **Total** ◯ **50**

Paper 20

The cost of some rides in the *Space Adventure Park* are:

Galaxy	£1.65	Laser	£2.80
Big Wheel	£1.45	Spaceship	£2.70

B 4
B 2

Amy went on two rides. She had £4.50 change from £10.

1–2 Which two rides did she go on? _____ and _____

John also went on two rides. He had £5.65 change from £10.

3–4 Which two rides did he go on? _____ and _____

5 How much would it cost to go on all four rides? _____

6 What is the **mean** price of a ride? _____

B 15
6

7 In the library there are 200 books. 58 of them are non-fiction.
What percentage of the books are non-fiction? _____

B 12
1

8–10 In Little Marsden the population is 17 222. The men and women together total 9142 and the women and children together total 13 201.

There are _____ women, _____ men and _____ children.

B 2
3

11 Take five hundred and sixty-seven from one thousand.
Write out your answer in figures. _____

B1/B2
1

Complete the figures below. The dotted line is the line of symmetry.

B 24

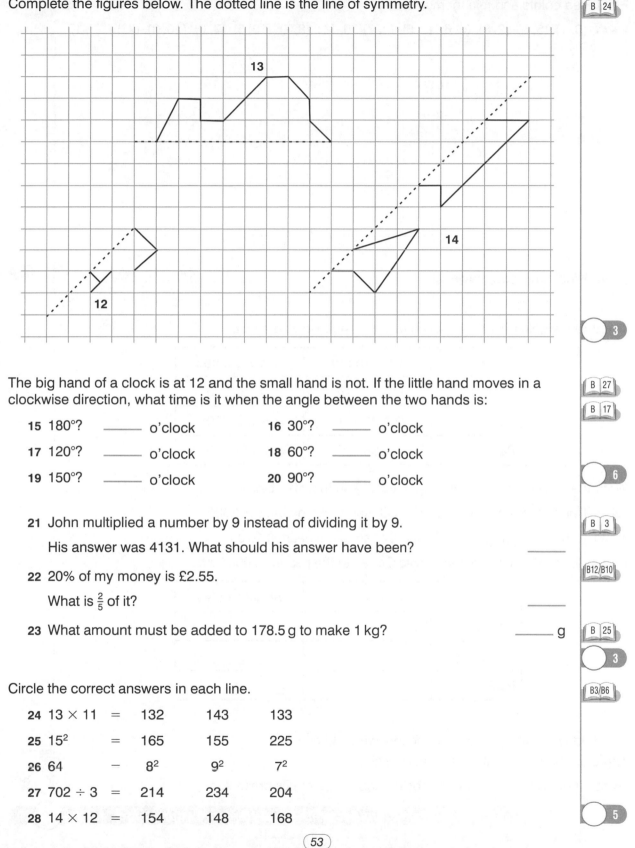

13

14

12

3

The big hand of a clock is at 12 and the small hand is not. If the little hand moves in a clockwise direction, what time is it when the angle between the two hands is:

B 27
B 17

15 180°? _____ o'clock   16 30°? _____ o'clock

17 120°? _____ o'clock   18 60°? _____ o'clock

19 150°? _____ o'clock   20 90°? _____ o'clock

6

21 John multiplied a number by 9 instead of dividing it by 9.

His answer was 4131. What should his answer have been? _____

B 3

22 20% of my money is £2.55.

What is $\frac{2}{5}$ of it? _____

B12/B10

23 What amount must be added to 178.5 g to make 1 kg? _____ g

B 25
3

Circle the correct answers in each line.

B3/B6

24 13 × 11 = 132   143   133

25 15^2 = 165   155   225

26 64 — 8^2 9^2 7^2

27 702 ÷ 3 = 214   234   204

28 14 × 12 = 154   148   168

5

Plot these points and join them in order.

29–41 (5, 1) (5, 5) (2, 3) (5, 6) (2, 5) (4, 7) (6, 11) (8, 7) (10, 5) (7, 6) (10, 3) (7, 5) (7, 1)

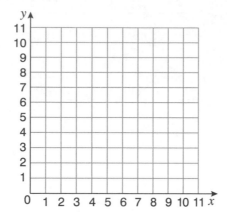

42 What have you drawn? _____

The three largest oceans in the world cover the following areas.

Ocean	Square km	Square miles
Atlantic	82 217 000	31 736 000
Indian	73 481 000	28 364 000
Pacific	165 384 000	63 838 000

Write the answers to the following questions in the table below.

43–44 Round the areas of the Atlantic Ocean to the nearest 100 000.

45–46 Round the areas of the Indian Ocean to the nearest 10 000.

47–48 Round the areas of the Pacific Ocean to the nearest 1 000 000.

Ocean	Square km	Square miles
Atlantic	_____	_____
Indian	_____	_____
Pacific	_____	_____

Last Friday $\frac{1}{8}$ of the pupils in our school were absent.
There are 560 pupils altogether in the school.

49–50 There were _____ pupils absent and _____ pupils present.

Now go to the Progress Chart to record your score!   Total   50

Paper 21

The products of the following calculations are either odd or even. Answer each question as either ODD or EVEN.

B 3

1 84 × 36 is an _____ number.

2 163 × 297 is an _____ number.

3 729 × 1468 is an _____ number.

4 292 × 36 × 52 is an _____ number.

4

Write the following amounts correct to the nearest £1.00.

B 1

5 £2.42 _____   **6** £2.71 _____   **7** £4.59 _____

8 £6.49 _____   **9** £7.50 _____

5

$\frac{2}{3}$ of a sum of money is 48p.

B 10

10 What is $\frac{5}{8}$ of the sum of money?   _____

1

Roast chicken must be cooked for 50 minutes per kg and then for an extra 20 minutes.

B 3

11–16 Complete this table of cooking times in hours and minutes.

Weight of chicken (kg)	Cooking time	
1	____ h	____ min
1.5	____ h	____ min
2	____ h	____ min
2.5	____ h	____ min
3	____ h	____ min
3.5	____ h	____ min

6

Divide these numbers by 1000.

B 1

17 374 _____   **18** 14.8 _____   **19** 2.55 _____

3

There are 420 children in a school. 45% of the pupils are boys.

B 12

20 How many boys are there?   _____

21 How many girls are there?   _____

2

£9.00 is shared between Amanda, Anita and Claire in the ratio of 8:5:2.

B 13

22 Amanda receives _____ .   **23** Anita receives _____ .   **24** Claire receives _____ .

3

25–29 Arrange these fractions in order, largest first.

$$\frac{7}{12} \qquad \frac{3}{8} \qquad \frac{3}{4} \qquad \frac{11}{24} \qquad \frac{5}{6}$$

_____ _____ _____ _____ _____

B 10

5

Suggest the best imperial unit to measure:

30 the distance from London to New York.   _____

31 the amount of water in a jug.   _____

32 the weight of a pencil.   _____

33 the height of a man.   _____

B 25

4

Convert these 24-hour clock times into a.m. 12-hour clock times.

| 20:20 | 08:05 | 00:10 | 17:45 |

32 _____   **35** _____   **36** _____   **37** _____

B 27

4

38–39 Add these children's ages.

	Years	Months
Zoe	10	11
Simon	10	8
David	11	4
Rachel	10	2
Tariq	10	8
Total		

B 2
B 15

40–41 What is their average age?   _____ years _____ months

4

Add the greatest value to the smallest.

42 £$\frac{1}{2}$ £0.55   27 × 2p   £$\frac{13}{25}$ £1.00 − 49p   _____

B10/B3
B 2

1

Scott has $\frac{1}{3}$ as many computer games as Anish, and Anish has $\frac{1}{2}$ as many games as Nick.
Together they have 140 games. How many do they have each?

43 Scott has _____ games.   **44** Anish has _____ games.   **45** Nick has _____ games.

B 10
B 13

3

We asked 72 children to name their favourite colour.
We made this pie chart.

B 14
B 3

46 How many children prefer green? _____

47 How many children prefer blue? _____

48 How many prefer orange? _____

49 How many like red best? _____

50 The number of children who prefer pink is _____

5

Now go to the Progress Chart to record your score! **Total** 50

Paper 22

The school hall is 4 times as long as it is wide.

B 20

1 If the perimeter is 55 m, what is the length? _____

2 What is the width? _____

2

Ahmed has 30 sweets; 60% of them are toffees and the rest are chocolates.

Ben has 40 sweets; $\frac{3}{8}$ of them are chocolates and the rest are toffees.

B 12
B 10
B 2

3 Who has the most toffees? _____

4–5 How many more than _____ does he have? _____

6 Who has the most chocolates? _____

7–8 He has _____ more than _____ .

6

Here are the number of music CDs these 6 friends had.

B 15

Name	Pete	Lucy	Kath	Jez	Helen	Simone
Number	8	5	14	19	14	12

9 What is the **mode**? _____ **10** What is the **median**? _____

11 What is the **range**? _____ **12** What is the **mean**? _____

4

Give the value of the 7 in each of the following numbers.

B 1

13 13.78 _____ **14** 37.89 _____ **15** 378.95 _____

3

1432 + 798 = 2230 so:

B 2

16 3432 + 798 will be _____

17 2432 + 1798 will be _____

18 4432 + 798 will be _____

3

Fill in the next two numbers in each line.

19–20	95	89	84	80	_____ _____
21–22	89	77	67	59	_____ _____
23–24	31	33	36	40	_____ _____
25–26	144	121	100	81	_____ _____

27–32 On the grid below, draw a bar chart to show the following information.

The number of cups of coffee sold at Buttercup Café last week:

Monday	90	Tuesday	110
Wednesday	70	Thursday	100
Friday	120	Saturday	140

Be careful to use a scale that will show this information accurately.

Write in your scale.

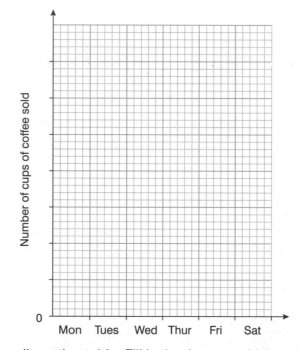

33–37 Here is part of a railway timetable. Fill in the times at which train B will reach the stations. It takes exactly the same time to do the journey as train A.

	Train A arrives at	Train B arrives at
Barwich	07:30	10:05
Hoole	07.48	_____
Carby	08.02	_____
Manton	08.15	_____
Pemby	08.29	_____
Durwich	08.54	_____

Your task is to guide the robot along the white squares on the plan.

It starts and finishes on one of the squares marked A, B, C, D or E.

It can only move FORWARD, turn RIGHT 90° and turn LEFT 90°.

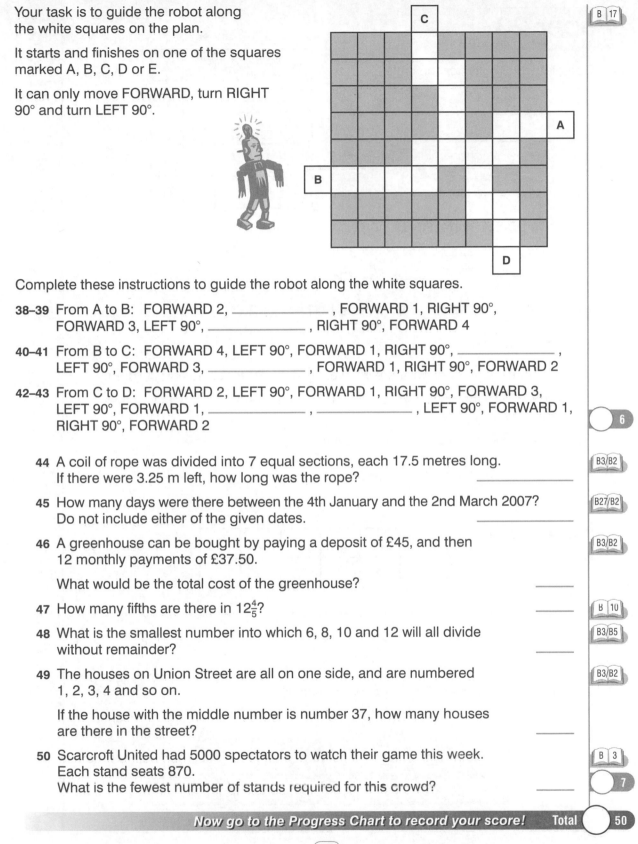

Complete these instructions to guide the robot along the white squares.

38–39 From A to B: FORWARD 2, _____ , FORWARD 1, RIGHT 90°, FORWARD 3, LEFT 90°, _____ , RIGHT 90°, FORWARD 4

40–41 From B to C: FORWARD 4, LEFT 90°, FORWARD 1, RIGHT 90°, _____ , LEFT 90°, FORWARD 3, _____ , FORWARD 1, RIGHT 90°, FORWARD 2

42–43 From C to D: FORWARD 2, LEFT 90°, FORWARD 1, RIGHT 90°, FORWARD 3, LEFT 90°, FORWARD 1, _____ , _____ , LEFT 90°, FORWARD 1, RIGHT 90°, FORWARD 2

6

44 A coil of rope was divided into 7 equal sections, each 17.5 metres long. If there were 3.25 m left, how long was the rope?   _____

B3/B2

45 How many days were there between the 4th January and the 2nd March 2007? Do not include either of the given dates.   _____

B27/B2

46 A greenhouse can be bought by paying a deposit of £45, and then 12 monthly payments of £37.50.

What would be the total cost of the greenhouse?   _____

B3/B2

47 How many fifths are there in $12\frac{4}{5}$?   _____

B 10

48 What is the smallest number into which 6, 8, 10 and 12 will all divide without remainder?   _____

B3/B5

49 The houses on Union Street are all on one side, and are numbered 1, 2, 3, 4 and so on.

If the house with the middle number is number 37, how many houses are there in the street?   _____

B3/B2

50 Scarcroft United had 5000 spectators to watch their game this week. Each stand seats 870. What is the fewest number of stands required for this crowd?   _____

B 3

7

Now go to the Progress Chart to record your score!   Total   50

59

Paper 23

1–10 Complete this multiplication table.

B 3

×				
	___	___	48	___
	___		30	___
	11	9	___	___
	66	___	___	24

Write the numbers below correct to the nearest 100.

11 71 246 _____

12 1486 _____

13 1274 _____

14 704.85 _____

15 What number is halfway between 98 and 144? _____

16–18 At Black Horse Junior School there were altogether 394 teachers and children.

The teachers and the boys numbered 189, and the girls and teachers together numbered 217.

There were _____ teachers, _____ boys and _____ girls.

19 Make 478 three hundred times as large. _____

20–23 Complete this table.

$\clubsuit = a + 3$

a	___	1	___	3
♣	3	___	5	___

Look in the circle and find the answers to these questions.

24 $9^2 - 8^2 =$ _____

25 $11^2 - 9^2 =$ _____

26 $2^3 + 2^2 =$ _____

27 $5^2 - 4^2 =$ _____

20 8
18 41
12 16 9
40 17

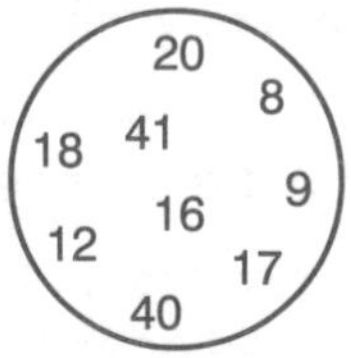

Find the area of these triangles. Scale: 1 square = 1 cm²

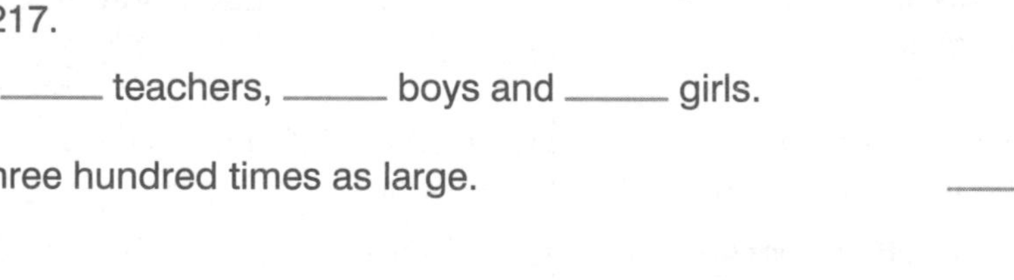

28 _____   **29** _____   **30** _____   **31** _____

Divide the year 2007 into 2 parts so that the second part is 4 times as large as the first part.

32 How many days are there in the shorter part? _____

33 In the larger part there are _____ days.

34 If the shorter part starts on January 1st, when does it end? _____

35 If $\frac{5}{12}$ of the contents of a box weigh 20 kg, what is the weight of all the contents? _____

36 What would $\frac{1}{8}$ of the contents weigh? _____

37–40 Fill in the missing numbers.

a	2	35	_____	47	_____
3a	6	_____	231	_____	267

41 By how much is the product of 27 and 13 greater than their sum? _____

There are 180 sheep in a flock. For every 9 white sheep there is 1 black sheep. How many:

42 white sheep are there? _____   **43** black sheep are there? _____

Mr Pin paid £7.05 for 1.5 metres of material.

44 What was the cost per metre? _____

45 How much would 3.5 m cost? _____

46 What is the next odd number after 160 into which 9 will divide without remainder? _____

47–50 Write these fractions in decimal form.

$3\frac{1}{8}$ $4\frac{1}{20}$ $7\frac{5}{8}$ $9\frac{3}{40}$ _____   _____   _____   _____

Now go to the Progress Chart to record your score!   Total   50

Paper 24

Underline the correct answer in each line.

1 $\frac{1}{3} + \frac{1}{4}$ = $\frac{1}{7}$ $\frac{7}{12}$ $\frac{2}{7}$ $\frac{2}{12}$

2 $10 - 1.99$ =   9.11   8.01   11.99   9.01

3 0.04×0.4 =   0.016   0.16   0.08   0.0016

4 $4 \div 0.02$ = 20 2 0.2 200

5 $17.89 \div 10$ = 178.9 1789 1.789 17.89

6 2.7×200 = 5.4 540 54.0 0.54

7 The perimeter of a square is 28 cm. What is its area? _____

8
$$\begin{array}{r} 147 \\ \times\ 49 \\ \hline \end{array}$$

_____

9–15 On the grid below draw a bar chart to show the information in the table. Be careful to use a scale which will show this information accurately. Write in your scale.

Shop	Cameras sold
A	225
B	75
C	150
D	175
E	300
F	125
G	200

Number of cameras sold

0 A B C D E F G

Shop

16 How many tiles, each 50 cm $\times$ 50 cm, would be needed to cover a floor 5 metres $\times$ 4 metres? _____

17 What would be the cost of these tiles if I had to pay £7.50 for 10 tiles? _____

18–19 Put a circle around the numbers which are not **prime numbers**.

3   13   23   33   43   53   63

20–23 What are the **factors** of 21?   ____ , ____ , ____ , ____

24–25 Underline the **prime factors** of 21.

2   3   4   5   6   7   8

26 How many times can 34 be subtracted from 986? _____

Ted has £98 and Tom has £64.

27 How much must Ted give to Tom so that they each have the same amount? _____

28 Would you estimate the number of children in a class to the nearest 10, 100, 1000? _____

29 Would you estimate the number of people at a Premier League football game to the nearest 10, 1000, 10 000 or 1 000 000? _____

30 The area of the flag is _____ .

31 The area of the cross is _____ .

32 The shaded part has an area of _____ .

33 The perimeter of the flag is _____ .

34 The perimeter of the cross is _____ .

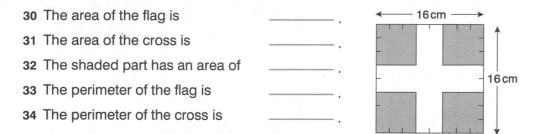

35–42 Complete the following table.

Fraction	Decimal	Percentage
$\frac{3}{10}$	_____	_____
$\frac{7}{100}$	_____	_____
_____	0.25	_____
$\frac{1}{20}$	_____	_____

43 8 − 1.127 = _____   44 47.625 ÷ 2.5 = _____

45–50 Complete the following table.

Wholesale price	Retail price	Profit
£18.75	£23.50	_____
_____	£70.20	£11.35
£5.13	_____	97p
£196.50	£235.25	_____
_____	£13.50	£2.19
93p	_____	19p

Progress Chart   Fourth papers in Maths

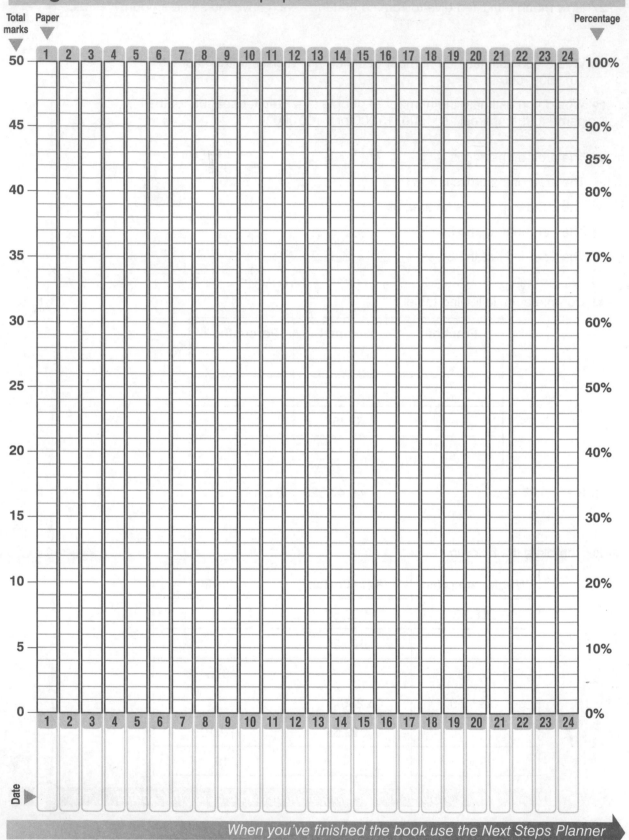

When you've finished the book use the Next Steps Planner